THE
REAL
DEAL

GET KNOWN FOR YOUR
GENUINE EXPERTISE IN AN
ERA OF BULLSH*T GURUS

MARY KATE GULICK

THE REAL DEAL
1st Edition 2020

Typesetting and layout design:
Shabbir Hussain (Access Ideas)

Free goodies, anyone?

Get my **33-Minute Weekly Social Media Planner** AND
Content Marketing Campaign Checklist now!

Join the **Real Deal Experts Creating Content
Facebook group** to access these two practical resources
and a whole lot of other free content. This is where I
spend most of my time, so I hope to see you there.

Join now at:
Facebook.com/groups/RealDealContent

· The ·
Content Goldmine
Weekly
Social Media
Planner

33 minutes a week.
3x the leads.

mary kate gulick

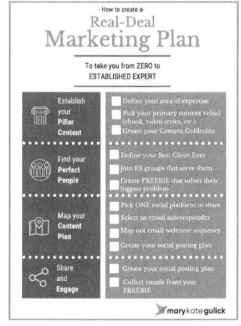

· How to create a-
Real-Deal
Marketing Plan

To take you from ZERO to
ESTABLISHED EXPERT

Establish your Pillar Content	Define your area of expertise
	Pick your primary content vehicle (ebook, video series, etc.)
	Create your Content Goldmine
Find your Perfect People	Define your Best Client Ever
	Join FB groups that serve them
	Create FREEBIE that solves their biggest problem
Map your Content Plan	Pick ONE social platform to share
	Select an email autoresponder
	Map out email welcome sequence
	Create your social posting plan
Share and Engage	Create your social posting plan
	Collect emails from your FREEBIE

mary kate gulick

ACKNOWLEDGEMENT

For Joshua, who supports all my bananas ideas and cheers me on as I run with them.

And to Jeannie Yandel, Nia Nielsen and Samantha Allen who provided me with invaluable feedback as I brought this over the finish line.

TABLE OF CONTENTS

INTRODUCTION

"The truth is, you need to be present on every social platform if you want to be taken seriously."

A total load of bullshit from a fake guru

The day I heard some non-expert on digital marketing chuck out this advice, I was floored. Wasn't he talking to entrepreneurs? People who were in the go-go-go days of building their own businesses? On what planet is it sustainable to have a robust presence on EVERY platform and still generate profit?

It was the first time I really noticed bad advice in the marketing space. And it made sense that I had missed it up to that point. The bulk of my two-decade marketing career had been spent in the company of agency creatives and successful corporate marketers—people who spent every day growing their own expertise in helping the companies they worked with get more clients, more exposure, and more revenue.

I didn't have a lot of exposure to "gurus" outside of the traditional marketing framework.

While I was a big fan of the democratization of knowledge that social media was, and the ability for anyone with expertise to step up and share what they knew to benefit others and grow a consulting business, on that particular day I saw for the first time that there are plenty of people with zero expertise hogging the mic.

And these Fake Gurus weren't just drowning out people with more experience and knowledge. They were making money (and a lot of it) from business owners who simply wanted to learn how to better get themselves out there.

Ew.

The worst part was, I remember thinking that there are plenty of Real Deal Experts out there. Good people with genuine expertise and a heart for teaching. Why weren't more of those people at the mic?

This wasn't just happening in marketing either. As I deliberately started paying attention, I was seeing Fake Gurus in life coaching, spirituality, parenting, business consulting, dog training . . .everywhere. And they were hogging the mic in their particular areas too. Why weren't the Real Deal Experts stepping up?

The more I started to dig into this question, the more I saw a disturbing trend. Real Deal Experts knew their specific areas of expertise inside and out. They just didn't necessarily feel comfortable with their ability to share that expertise on a broad scale and push for the visibility they deserved.

Fake Gurus vs. Real Deal Experts

When I talk about "Fake Gurus," I'm specifically referencing people who woke up one sunny day and decided they wanted to make money online without doing a ton of work. So they signed up for a class on Instagram monetization or became a ClickFunnels affiliate or joined a Law of Attraction Facebook group—then immediately started calling themselves an Instagram Success Coach or Funnel Expert or Life Coach.

And all this with no credentials.
No experience.
And no genuine expertise to share.

Their goal was to repurpose the content they learned in a course or from an affiliate, pass it off as their own, and make bank off unsuspecting consumers and entrepreneurs who wished for a real-life transformation.

Again, ew.

If you want the ultimate example of a Fake Guru, think of Kenneth Branagh's portrayal of Gilderoy Lockhart in *Harry Potter and the Chamber of Secrets.* He stole the accomplishments of better wizards and passed them off as his own. And his lack of genuine know-how caused big problems for anyone who actually needed help.

(NOTE: If you and I haven't spent any time together yet, you'll need to get used to me reaching for Harry Potter references as my go-to for teaching. It's a fandom that pretty much illustrates everything worth knowing as a human being. I'm happy to get into lengthy arguments on this point.)

You can see the danger in this, right? We're at a time when everyone—moms, teachers, entrepreneurs, furloughed employees, newly-minted homeschoolers, homebound professionals, people trying to maintain their health in terrifying times—need help figuring some things out and making life better. If the only people to turn to are phonies, what kind of advice will they get? What kind of money will they sink into some blowhard that provides zero useful guidance?

That's why Real Deal Experts are so critical. The Real Deal Expert is the polar opposite of a Fake Guru.

The Real Deal Expert wakes up and says, "Hey, I know more about this topic than just about anyone. I've been successfully doing it for a long time, people in the industry respect my opinion, and I'm appropriately credentialed. I bet there are other people out there who could use this knowledge to improve their lives or businesses. I wonder what the best way is to connect with them?"

There are a few distinct differences. First, and most obviously, the Real Deal Expert actually knows what the hell she's talking about.

Second, the focus of the Real Deal Expert is on sharing expertise to help people. Yes, she wants to make money from her expertise knowledge (as she should), but she knows the kind of money she wants to make comes from providing value and solving problems.

A Note About Traditional Credentials

It is not lost on me that many college and post-graduate degrees, membership in certain professional societies, structured awards, etc., are not equally available to everyone. Economic inequity and systemic racism are still at work, throwing up barriers to these traditional credentials. Non-traditional credentials, such as lower-cost certifications, testimonials from those you have helped, case studies of the work you have done, are just as (if not even more) critical in showcasing your Real Deal status. When I talk about credentials, I don't just mean having the right letters after your name. For some fields (therapists, for example) those letters are required. For many other fields, informal credentials do the trick.

Our Fake Guru, on the other hand, is primarily focused on the money, and views the knowledge he is "borrowing" from others as a means to that end. There's no focus on providing value or solving problems . . . just tricking people into thinking that he knows something that they don't.

What does our Fake Guru have that our Real Deal Expert doesn't? A boatload of confidence and a good sense of how to sell on social media. That's it.

So my viewpoint is this: If more Real Deal Experts had the same confidence as their Fake Guru counterparts, and had a solid content strategy in place to put themselves out there, more of them could get up to the mic. There would be more good advice in the world. And more people would get the real help they needed.

Real Deal Experts and Imposter Syndrome

I've often struggled with using the "Fake Guru" and "Real Deal Expert" dichotomy. More than once, I've had Real Deal Experts say to me that they think they're actually Fake Gurus.

These are people who have been living and breathing their area of expertise for 10, 15, and 20-plus years, helping clients, gaining a deep understanding that only significant experience can bring. THESE are the people who worry they might be Fake Gurus.

(Please know that an actual Fake Guru would never worry about not knowing enough. This is simply not a concern to them.)

I've seen it over and over again:

> "Mary Kate, you keep calling me an expert, but I'm not comfortable with that. Maybe 'specialist' is a better term for me?"

"Yes, I have my certification and an MA in the subject. Yes, I've been doing it for 22 years. But am I really and EXPERT expert?"

"I know you only work with people with deep expertise, and I'm worried that's not me. I've been doing this for 17 years, yes, but now I'm focusing on a different audience, so . . ."

Y'all . . . I don't know whether to laugh or cry when I hear exceedingly competent, profoundly qualified, and deeply seasoned people talking about themselves like they have no right to claim expert status.

These are people who are so submerged in their own expertise that it just feels like "common sense" to them. Everybody knows this stuff really, right?

Nope. YOU know this stuff like you were born to it because you are an expert. And the failure of Real Deal Experts to recognize this has contributed to the mass of Fake Gurus and bullshit advice across nearly every vertical.

So, if you're a Real Deal Expert who thinks that you're not, please read this carefully:

THE WORLD NEEDS YOU RIGHT NOW.
EXPERTISE MATTERS.
EXPERIENCE MATTERS.

Without experts who truly know what they're talking about, we're all doomed to keep listening to the only people who step up to the mic. If you know your stuff, you owe it to all of us to share it. To step up to the microphone and drown out the ill-informed, hyped-up fluff that's being pushed our way.

Who the hell am I, anyway?

All this talk about Real Deal Experts and Fake Gurus begs the question: Which one am I? I'm not shy about claiming my Real Deal Expert status.

I started my first job as a copywriter at a mid-sized ad agency in 2001, so at the time of writing this, I've been creating marketing content, building content strategies, and advising on brand messaging strategies for nearly 20 years.

In those two decades, I've been at advertising and digital agencies, in the marketing departments of Fortune 500 companies (IBM and TD Ameritrade), and even a stint at a scrappy midwestern nonprofit focused on preventing child abuse.

I've won awards and made money for lots of great companies. And along the way, I've always done "side work" with independent entrepreneurs—therapists, caregivers, consultants, advisors, coaches, trainers, freelance designers, photographers— the full monty.

In the fall of 2019, I learned that the company I loved, TD Ameritrade, was being acquired by a larger brokerage. This meant that my dream job would likely be evaporating over the next few years.

After I got over the total gut-punch of the news (and a fair bit of ugly crying), it occurred to me that having time to figure out what I wanted my life to look like before my position was eliminated— almost a full year prior—was the biggest gift I had ever received. How often do you get that kind of warning before a major life change? So, I got down to the work of figuring out what I was meant to do.

I worked with my personal life coach, my business coach, and my leadership coach to figure out what the hell to do with my life. Who was I when I wasn't an executive-level digital and content marketing leader at a Fortune 500 company? Isn't that what I've worked for over the last 20 years? Where was my value if I wasn't leading at that level?

There was the idea of relocating for another high-level corporate position. The headhunters were out in full force getting all kinds of opportunities in front of me. But the truth was I did NOT WANT to move. I love Omaha (my Homaha), my kids love their schools, and my parents had just moved from Chicago to be closer to us. Relocating was not part of the equation.

As I worked with my coaches, it started to become clear that the idea of taking another corporate job sounded awful to me. It just repelled me so viscerally that I finally simply stopped thinking of it as a possibility.

The only possibilities I was interested in would allow me to:

1) Lead a high-quality, close-knit creative team that does purpose-driven work.

2) Individually teach Real Deal Experts how to get in front of more people.

It became evident that I needed two jobs—not just one. As soon as I got clarity on that, what I now needed to do, I started getting giddy. All the uncertainty I experienced after the acquisition announcement fell away, and my path lay wide open in front of me.

So as I started thinking through possibilities to lead a creative team, I also opened my own business, Real Deal Content Coaching. My main goal was to teach Real Deal Experts to turn all the deep know-how in their brains into compelling online content that builds their brand as a thought leader and drives leads their way.

In short, I wanted to give Real Deal Experts a big and loud flipping microphone.

So 20 years in, I've done it all. I know what works for corporations and how those plans do NOT work for solo entrepreneurs. And I know that the approach you employ to promote genuine expertise is not the same approach if you're just a Fake Guru trying to sell some nonsense you scrounged from someone else.

The point of this book

I wrote this book as a step-by-step guide for experts, consultants, coaches, advisors and service providers who are committed to using their deep expertise to help others. As I write this in the middle of the coronavirus lockdown, it has never been so certain how much people need experts like you.

- Everyone who's been laid off or furloughed needs career and life coaches to figure out where to go next and financial advisors to help them figure out how to deal with the money situations that have come up.

- All those new businesses that have just started to need marketing consultants and business coaches to scale quickly.

- Those with amped-up depression and anxiety need therapists and counselors.

- All of us who are eating our feelings day in and day out need nutritionists and health coaches.

- Since we can't go to the gym, we need our fitness coaches to help us stay in shape at home.

- Parents who are spending more time together with their kids, and keeping them occupied without going out, need parenting coaches and homeschooling experts.

- Marriages that are straining under unprecedented stress need relationship counselors.

- Everyone needs more creativity and spirituality in their lives.

- Pet owners who decided now would be an AWESOME time to buy a dog need dog trainers.

You get the idea. We've never needed each other more. We've never needed experts like YOU more. And if you don't believe that you can do good for your community and serve the people who need your expertise AND ALSO be paid what you're worth for what you know, this is probably not the book for you. This book is here to give you everything you need to know to build an expertise-focused content marketing plan so you can build your personal brand, establish yourself as a thought leader, and attract the right kind of clients to your business.

We'll do this together by:

- Getting a clear understanding of Content Marketing as a discipline.

- Developing a crystal-clear picture of your ideal client.

- Committing to a brand messaging strategy so it's obvious who you are and what you're about.

- Setting up a Minimum Viable Content Experience so you can get yourself out there and learn from your audience while you're building out your larger-scale content.

- Creating your Content Goldmine—a big, meaty, thud-worthy piece of content that showcases the depth of your expertise.

- Mining your Content Goldmine for frequent content volume without needing an agency or marketing department.

- Determining the one to two social media and distribution platforms that are best for you so you're not spinning your wheels on platforms that don't matter to your audience.

- Nurturing each lead that comes in the door with an authentic, action-driving email.

I'm genuinely thrilled that you've included me in your content journey as a Real Deal Expert. I truly believe that if we can put the microphone in front of more people who really know their stuff, and get more high-quality advice out to businesses and families, we can make a massive impact on people's wealth, happiness and overall quality of life.

CHAPTER 1:
Content Marketing 101

In high-trust areas like coaching and consulting, Content Marketing is the most effective strategy for building trust with prospects, generating qualified leads, and nurturing those leads to become clients.

Corporate businesses have the benefit of advertising agency partners and marketing departments on their side to generate the volume of content required. For Real Deal Experts who are just getting started, replicating this volume can be the biggest challenge. The model in this chapter is designed specifically for solo, service-based entrepreneurs to generate the necessary volume in a way that's 100% authentic to who you are, sustainable, automatable and scalable.

Content Marketing Defined

There are multiple definitions of Content Marketing as a discipline floating around in the world. The one I regard as the most accurate and most useful to those building personal thought leadership brands comes from the Content Marketing Institute.

> **Content Marketing is a strategic marketing approach focused on creating and distributing valuable, relevant, and consistent content to attract and retain a clearly defined audience — and, ultimately, to drive profitable customer action**

I like this definition for a reason. Within it, you'll find all the guidance necessary to create a Content Marketing program that matters to the people you're trying to serve, and that meets your goals as a business. Let's unpack it.

Strategic marketing approach: Common to the practice that we see by many inexperienced businesses, Content Marketing is not about creating a volume of content for its own sake. As a strategic marketing approach, the content created within effective content marketing programs is tied to specific goals.

- What idea do I want to own in the marketplace?
- How do I best build trust with my ideal prospects?
- What are my ideal prospects most interested in right now?
- What content is required to move someone from interested to taking action?

Every piece of content within a Content Marketing program under this definition has a strategic business purpose—either establishing a connection, deepening the relationship, moving to a first sale, or generating repeat business.

Creating and distributing: All of the action on your part within a Content Marketing program lies in the creation and distribution of content. For the creation, you're looking at any combination of:

- Landing pages
- Blog posts
- Videos
- Podcasts/audio files
- eBooks/white papers
- Webinars
- Worksheets
- Calculators/tools
- Checklists, cheat sheets or other downloadables
- Infographics
- Courses/Learning series
- Emails
- Social media posts

Which type of content you decide to create is wholly up to you. Maybe the idea of stepping in front of the camera makes you want to fake your own death. Or the idea of writing a 40-page eBook gives you the queasies. The goal is to find the content formats that you can do CONSISTENTLY and become really proficient at.

There are a few on here that are non-negotiables, however.

- Social media posts: This is the primary means of distribution to find new content consumers.

- Landing pages: You'll use landing pages to collect email addresses for certain pieces of high-value content. This is the mechanism by which you'll build your email list.

- Email: You'll use email to distribute content to known contacts, but more importantly, email will be the primary way you move known contacts to paying client status.

Valuable: The content you'll be producing is educational, enlightening and helpful. It provides value to your ideal prospect by providing information that they need. Generally, this means the content is NOT highly promotional in nature but is meant to solve a problem. Most of your content will improve the user's life and ask nothing in return (except perhaps an email address).

Relevant: Your content is not generic, and is not meant to solve problems for each and everyone. It addresses a specific set of problems and concerns held by your clearly defined audience. Relevant content shows up at the right time in a prospect's life, often based on what she's searching for online. Relevant content is 100% about the prospect and her problem. It is not about you. Because you've answered a question and solved a problem, relevant content builds a connection and trust between you and the prospect.

Consistent: Your content needs to be there when your prospect needs it—not when you feel like getting around to it. That means you'll require frequent publication. Your unique brand voice should be recognizable and consistently applied. And your content should be easy to find whenever a prospect needs it.

Clearly defined audience: In order to create content that is valuable, relevant, and consistent, you need to clearly define who you're talking to. What are the unique characteristics of your audience? What are the problems they're trying to solve? What are the search terms they're using to solve those problems?

All too often for experts who want to turn their know-how into a business, the focus is more on what you can offer and less on the client who needs it. Unless we clearly define the audience we're talking to, the content we create will be generic, irrelevant and without value.

Seriously, take the time to do this. The whole of the next chapter is dedicated specifically to defining the audience you're planning to work with.

Drive profitable customer action: We're not creating all this content for our health, y'all. While everyone loves an audience, the goal of a Content Marketing program is to grow an audience with the intent of converting those eyeballs into paying clients. So it's not enough to provide content that solves problems. The goal is to systematically pull those newly connected prospects deeper into your knowledge ecosystem so they recognize you as the one who can solve their problem, then consistently provide them with opportunities to work with you so you can change their lives.

Why Content Marketing

When it comes to high-trust businesses, Content Marketing is the most effective way to connect with new prospects and convert them into clients at scale. Period.

And if you're reading this book, it's because you have deep expertise you want to share with clients in exchange for money. You're asking clients to believe that you have the knowledge and ability to help them make a dramatic change in their lives, health, relationships or businesses. By definition, you're in a high-trust business.

So how do we know that Content Marketing works? Fortunately for us, there have been plenty of large companies and tech start-ups who have put the research in for us over the last 10 years. Here's what we know for sure:

Consumers want high-quality content

In the last 20 years, the search engine has become the primary go-to for all questions—big and small. Consumers have come to expect that results will answer their specific questions in a way that is most relevant to them. And most of this relevant content? It comes from businesses who were smart enough to take the time to figure out what their prospects wanted. And because of this, consumers have developed more trust for content they perceive as educational than traditional advertising.

According to Demand Metric, 70% of consumers would rather learn from products in an article or blog than an ad. The format has more credibility and context and is more focused on solving a specific problem for the consumer.

A recent Animoto study shares that 73% of consumers have been influenced by a brand's social media presence prior to purchase. And Hubspot's recent research shows that 87% of consumers are straight-up asking for more videos from brands. It's their preferred way of learning about products and how they can solve problems.

Content Marketing drives more leads for less

There's a reason Content Marketing has become the primary strategy by which high-trust and business-to-business companies drive leads into their funnel. Because it works and it costs a whole lot less.

The Content Marketing Institute shares that effective Content Marketing programs drive 3x more leads than traditional advertising. And those leads cost 62% less than the ones that come from traditional ad programs. These numbers alone make it obvious that Content Marketing is a requirement for any business—large or small—that needs a steady lead flow.

Another study from Kapost/Oracle found that on average, Content Marketing leads cost 41% less than leads generated by paid search. A study by IMPACT found that brands that blog consistently saw 126% more lead growth than brands that don't. Blogs in general drive significantly higher organic search traffic to their producers' websites. TechClient noted in a recent study that websites with blog content have 424% more search indexed pages than those without. And overall, effective Content Marketers get 7.8x more organic search traffic than their competitors (Aberdeen).

And what happens with all that traffic and all those leads? According to Aberdeen, those who adopt effective Content Marketing practices see a 6x higher conversion rate than those who don't.

So the lesson is pretty clear on this one. Need more leads for less? Want them to convert better? Adopt a Content Marketing approach.

Content Marketing makes prospects more likely to trust you

It's not just about the number of eyeballs that an effective Content Marketing program puts on your work, but it's the quality of those eyeballs. Users who find you through useful content are more likely to trust you, see you as having their best interest at heart, and think of you as a go-to for information about the topic.

In fact, in a recent Contently survey, the company found that 47% of millennials are more likely to trust a financial services firm that produced useful content. I selected this example for a reason—financial services are frequently cited as the least trusted industry in the United States. Knowing that nearly half of a massive generation is willing to trust a financial services firm just based on content is very telling indeed.

In the same study, Contently determined that 56% of consumers surveyed trust brand-created content more than traditional media outlets. This (somewhat disturbing) fact illuminates the impact that problem-solving, relevant, high-value content can have on your ideal clients.

Audience ownership vs. audience rental

This is what I consider the most compelling reason to adopt a Content Marketing strategy consistently as a way to build trust and market your expertise-based business. When you rely on paid sources of promotion—whether that's Facebook ads, paid search, or whatever—you're essentially renting an audience. You'll generate leads as long as you pay for them. But when you stop paying, those leads dry up.

When you're investing your time and expertise into Content Marketing, you're putting content out into the world that will be out there forever, solving problems for clients, and driving them deeper into your ecosystem. This chart, created by the Content Marketing Institute, illustrates the power of owning an audience over time, versus rending via paid channels.

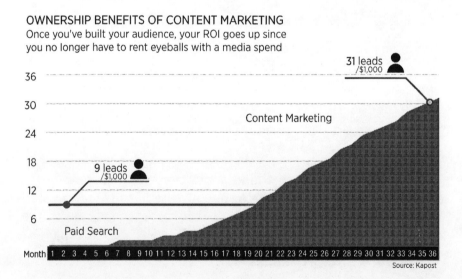

OWNERSHIP BENEFITS OF CONTENT MARKETING
Once you've built your audience, your ROI goes up since you no longer have to rent eyeballs with a media spend

In this example, as long as you're paying the $1,000/month in paid search, you'll get nine leads per month. That doesn't vary. But as you start producing content, each month you build the number of leads, you're able to produce from that content. The volume of content compounds and the leads generated become far greater than what your paid search budget would allow you to reach.

Requirements for Success

If you're with me so far, you're on board with the idea that Content Marketing is a proven way to build trust, generate leads, and convert sales.

Great. Now how do we do it successfully?

Generally speaking, there are three requirements for the success of a Content Marketing program:

Validation:

Your content should focus on topics that have been VALIDATED to be of interest to your clients. We can discover these topics by looking at search data, and engaging with our audiences in several systematic ways. More on this in the next chapter. Content pieces should be built around validated search terms so your content can be there for clients when they're looking for it.

Velocity:

Your content should be designed for every different stage in the customer life cycle, each focused on moving them to the next stage. By mapping out these stages at the beginning, you can build your content to increase VELOCITY from introduction to deal close.

Volume:

This means exactly what it sounds like. You do want a lot of content. Not a lot for the sake of volume itself, but a lot surrounding the validated topics you want to own. That's how you grow your domain authority and start becoming known—by humans and search engines alike—for your area of expertise.

Large corporations and even mid-sized B2B companies have the luxury of marketing departments and advertising agencies to produce volume for them. You don't.

So how can a solo expert produce the kind of volume that's required for success? Enter the Content Goldmine.

The Content Goldmine Model

Simply put, the Content Goldmine Model allows a solo expert, coach or consultant without a marketing team or massive advertising budget to create the volume of high-quality content required to run a successful Content Marketing program. It allows you to do it quickly, consistently, and in a way that establishes and magnifies your expertise while generating leads.

Here's how the model works:

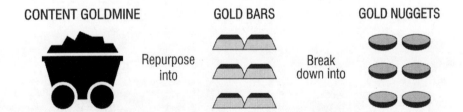

CONTENT GOLDMINE   GOLD BARS   GOLD NUGGETS

Repurpose into   Break down into

The Content Goldmine

The first, most critical piece of the system is the Content Goldmine. This is a big, meaty, thud-worthy content piece that houses all of your expertise and what makes it unique. It's where you share your philosophy, framework, research, experiences, exercises and encouragement. Examples of Content Goldmines include:

- Ultimate Guide eBooks
- How-To eBooks
- Original Research Reports
- Online Courses
- Real Books

In Chapter 5, we'll jump right into how to create your Content Goldmine quickly, and which type you should work on.

The purpose of the Goldmine piece is three-fold:

1. It proves and showcases your expertise.
2. It acts as the engine for the rest of your content through strategic repurposing.
3. It serves as the ultimate "lead magnet," allowing you to exchange it for an email address and to potentially charge for it, generating low-ticket customers.

Gold Bars

Gold bar content is sections of your Content Goldmine, repurposed for different formats, including:

- Blog Posts

- Videos

- Infographics

- Webinars

- Worksheets

- Checklists

- Quizzes

Much of this content (blog posts, videos and infographics) are ungated content, allowing your ideal prospects to find it via search engines when they're looking to solve a problem. Other pieces (webinars, worksheets, checklists, quizzes, some videos, etc.) are gated, meaning your prospect will need to provide you with an email address in order to access the asset.

The three purposes of Gold Bar content are to:

- Introduce people to your brand via search.

- Push people to the Content Goldmine.

- Exchange content for an email address.

Gold Nuggets

Gold Nugget content is the social posts and emails that distribute your other content. The purpose of Gold Nuggets is to introduce people to your brand through social media sharing, in communities that they're already familiar with, and to expand their relationship with your content through email.

Here's what the Content Goldmine Model looks like in action:

As an example, let's say the Content Goldmine, in this case, was an Ultimate Guide-style eBook.

Each subsection can be broken down into a blog post, netting **48 blog posts,** each of which can be prescheduled and optimized to rank for relevant search terms.

The author decides to make each of the 3 main sections into **3 webinars** that she'll spread out throughout the year.

There are multiple statistics within 4 different sections, so the author creates **4 infographics.**

There are several concepts in the book that the author considers foundational, so she creates **6 short videos**, one illustrating each concept. She shoots these all in an hour and has a VA edit and upload them.

The eBook has **8 worksheets and 3 checklists** as part of it, so the author extracts each of these for use as a separate lead magnet.

Finally, the author decides to create a **quiz** around some of her concepts that is a fun, interactive way for users to learn.

Altogether, this Content Goldmine has yielded 69 separate pieces of Gold Bar content. A blog post for nearly every week of the year, quarterly infographics, and gated lead magnets, webinars and quizzes to collect email addresses more than once per month.

Don't even get me started on the nuggets . . .

No, let's do get started on it. Because it just gets exponential from here.

Each of the 48 blog posts is promoted with a post social media upon publication, then again 6 months after publication (96 social posts).

Because each of the 4 infographic shows multiple data points, each infographic easily yields 5 separate graphics to serve as eye-catching social media graphics that link to the larger infographic for full context (20 social posts).

Each short video can be shown on its own via social media (6 social posts).

Each worksheet and checklist downloadable is promoted via live video and 4 posts via social media (60 social posts).

The webinars are promoted 5 times each via social media (15 social posts).

The quiz is promoted 3 times via social media (3 social posts).

Add to that a weekly email newsletter to your list that promotes the weekly blog post, shares whatever gold bars are most relevant at the time, and sells your paid offer, and you're consistently leading people deeper into your content ecosystem (52 emails).

With Gold Bars and Gold Nuggets accounted for, you're looking at 321 pieces of content. Before you start having a panic attack, remember this: NONE OF IT IS NEW CONTENT. Every one of those 321 pieces comes directly from your Content Goldmine. It's just slightly tweaked and repurposed for a new format.

Now take a breath. Is it worth spending some time producing one big piece to get that much content out of it for the year?

Why the Content Goldmine Works for Personal Brands

For experts, coaches and consultants who don't have an advertising agency or a marketing staff to produce the volume required to generate real thought leadership within their areas of expertise, the Content Goldmine Model gets the job done. The above example makes the case for volume, but that's not the only reason the model works well for personal brands.

It focuses your story

Because every one of the Gold Bar and Gold Nugget pieces of content comes directly from the Content Goldmine, all of your content is concentrated around your area of expertise. There's no randomness, no fluff, no wasted content. Every word and pixel you publish is reinforcing your core story and building the case around you as an expert.

Search juice

With this kind of volume focused on one core topic and framework, you're building genuine domain authority with search engines. The blog on your website is helping the search engines recognize your dot-com as the go-to spot for your area of expertise. The more you share this content and it's shared by others, the more backlinks you'll generate to your site, increasing your domain authority and standing as an expert with search engines even more. The more relevant, high-quality content you publish in different formats—even if it's repurposed from your PDF—the more search juice you'll enjoy, the more organic traffic you'll get, and the more leads you'll be able to generate.

It's just less work

Now we get into the behavioral bit of it. Constantly churning out new, innovative content and always having to generate new ideas is unsustainable for an entrepreneur who's just getting started. Most of your time should be dedicated to clients and sales. The goal of the Content Goldmine Model is to create a sustainable, manageable, and even fully outsource-able Content Marketing program. The truth is that once your Content Goldmine piece is complete, the name of the game is copy, paste, tweak, schedule, and repeat.

CHAPTER 1 - **SUMMARY**

- *Content Marketing is a strategic marketing approach focused on creating and distributing valuable, relevant, and consistent content to attract and retain a clearly defined audience—and, ultimately, to drive profitable customer action. (Content Marketing Institute.)*

- *Content Marketing makes prospects more willing to trust you.*

- *Content Marketing generates more leads for less and converts more of those leads than traditional advertising or paid search.*

- *In order to be successful, your Content Marketing program needs validation of what the prospect actually cares about, velocity through your sales funnel, and volume of content.*

- *The Content Goldmine Model allows solo experts, coaches and consultants to achieve massive volume with a small amount of work.*

NOTES

CHAPTER 2:

Your Best. Client. Ever!

You may have heard the old saying: When you market to everyone, you sell to no one. It's true, today more than ever!

Your expertise might provide an amazing transformation for a broad swath of people. But as you're building your service-based business, the best approach is to focus on the narrow audience that needs, wants, and can benefit most from what you have to offer. Nail that audience down, perfect your message and offering, then expand.

Let's dive into finding your Best. Client. Ever!

Defining Your Audience

In the last chapter, we talked about some of the key words in the definition of Content Marketing.

> Content Marketing is a strategic marketing approach focused on creating and distributing valuable, relevant, and consistent content to **attract and retain a clearly defined audience** — and, ultimately, to drive profitable customer action.

If the goal of the content you're creating is to attract and retain a clearly-defined audience, we first need to clearly define that audience. There are multiple ways to do this—both qualitative and quantitative. The goal is that by working through the advice in this chapter, you'll have a crystal clear understanding of who your ideal client is, what she's struggling with, what she wants, what she's afraid of, and what she's willing to do to reach her goals.

Let's start by scratching the surface and understanding who's in your Best. Client. Ever! group.

3, 4, 5 Layers Deep

I once asked a Financial Advisor who his Best. Client. Ever! was. Do you know what he said?

"Anyone with money."

And he wondered why his competitors who were dialed into millennial doctors and retiring law enforcement officers were clobbering him in performance.

When we looked deeper into his favorite clients, it allowed us to better understand who he best served . . . because of his offering, demeanor and how he was perceived in the marketplace. It even came as a surprise to him.

We looked at his favorite clients. What did they have in common? What drew them to him? Why were they his favorites? What made him enjoy working with these clients above others?

As it turned out, one handful of his favorite clients all worked for the same enormous company in his metropolitan area. They still had an old-time defined benefit pension plan and were either retired or in the process of retiring. So for the medium-term, that audience was retirement-age professionals leaving company X. Because that audience was so specific, he could speak directly to their unique questions and problems, and market to them in highly unique and targeted ways (events in conjunction with the company's benefits department, targeted LinkedIn outreach based on present and past company, etc.).

But this wasn't an audience that would last forever—even now, the company was doing away with its defined benefit pension plan. So we looked at another handful of favorites, that on the surface, didn't seem to have that much in common.

Some were entrepreneurs. Some were high-paid executives.

Some were in their 30s. Some were in their 50s.

Some lived in the city. Some lived in the suburbs.

What they all had in common was they were outliers in terms of their level of ambition and success, and they were extremely hands-off with their long-term wealth management. They were all high earners with no plans to stop any time soon. They were all deeply involved with their professional communities and traveled for work frequently. They all had busy families. Every one of these clients was run-off-their-feet busy. They were also particularly relieved to delegate that work to someone else and were incredibly grateful for the services that the advisor provided.

This was an audience the advisor could tap into for years to come. This was an audience he could build a practice around.

When we look at this audience one level deep, we see that they're full-time professionals.

When we look two levels deep, we see that they're high earning.

When we look three levels deep, we see that they're among the most ambitious and high-performing professionals out there.

When we look four levels deep, we see that they have a rich and very busy family life.

When we look five levels deep, we see that they believe financial planning is critical, but it is something they have zero interest in taking on themselves and are willing to pay for full stewardship.

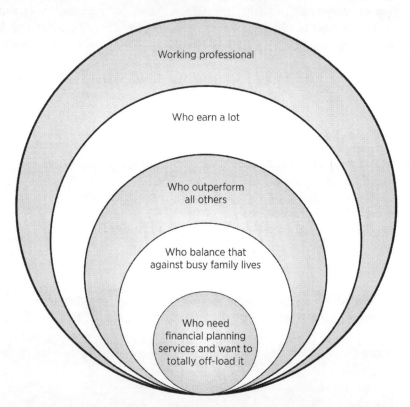

When the advisor looked at this, it caused him to question his offering. He had been really leaning into consulting only services for those who wanted to hold and trade their own investments, as well as a lot of education about investments. This audience? They just wanted to turn over the keys and pop in every year to be assured that things were alright.

This was a revelation when it came to his messaging. He needed to be focusing on how he would remove the stress of financial management, take the guesswork out of financial decisions, and offer certainty when it came to making sure things were done the right way. Had he not gone 5 levels deep here, he never would have nailed that messaging and would have continued targeting "Everyone with money" with very little success.

I went through this with my own audience. Obviously, I work with entrepreneurs who have an online business. But if that was the only way I defined my audience, it would be so huge and varied, I would have a difficult time nailing down those relevant messaging points that would really resonate. Here's what my 5 levels deep looks like.

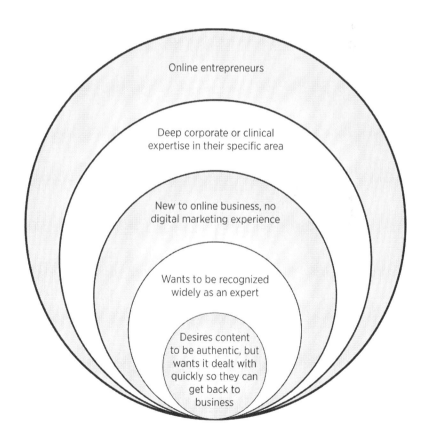

Online entrepreneurs

Deep corporate or clinical expertise in their specific area

New to online business, no digital marketing experience

Wants to be recognized widely as an expert

Desires content to be authentic, but wants it dealt with quickly so they can get back to business

This level of clarity was enormously helpful for me. The messaging for someone who is new to the digital marketing space is dramatically different than it is for a veteran. While my clients are veterans in their respective Nerd Zones, the whole concept of content creation, repurposing, and distribution was new to them. And you know what? They're mildly interested in the process, but more than anything, just want it dealt with so they can work with clients. That's what they really care about. They don't want to be content experts.

I would still be trying to sell them a path to content expertise if I hadn't gone 5 levels deep.

What are your five levels deep for your audience?

Feeling the Pain

Chances are, just given your area of expertise, you probably already know quite a bit about your Best. Client. Ever!—their experiences and their problems. But like anyone else, over time, we lose touch with some of that understanding as we solve the problem and get farther away from it.

Fortunately, it takes just a little empathy to reconnect with our Best. Client. Ever! Just take a few minutes to join them in what I like to call the "Pit of Despair."

Yeah, I definitely stole that from *The Princess Bride*.

For our purposes, the Pit of Despair is the lowest of the low that your Best. Client. Ever! can get when it comes to the problem that you're planning to solve for them. What does that look like?

- How is your client feeling?

- What's stopping her from moving forward?

- What is she feeling guilty about in how she's living?

- What is the dream or desire she has that she'd be ashamed of if anyone knew?

- What is she afraid will happen? What keeps her up at night?

- What does she know she has to do but doesn't know how to move forward?

- On the flip side, what does she daydream about? What does she dream her life will look like one day?

- What is the thing she wants so desperately but doesn't believe it's possible because she's in the Pit of Despair?

- What will life look like if nothing changes?

Spend some time answering these questions and sit with these emotions. Write down what it feels like as this client . . . to be down in that Pit of Despair. How does it feel emotionally, physically? When we get into developing the components of your brand message in the next chapter, we'll use much of this language.

To get insights into this, spend time in Facebook groups where your ideal client is hanging out. They'll talk about their troubles there. You'll see what kind of language they use, what solutions they've tried, and what the Pit of Despair looks like. Check out Quora to see what kind of questions they're asking around their problems. Visit subreddits on their main problem and look at those conversations.

For the advisor who we were talking about above, his Best. Client. Ever! had a sinking, ever-present feeling that he was spending every cent that came in. He felt like he was running a race he couldn't win because he couldn't out-earn his own busy, chaotic life. With all the power moves made earlier in his career, he'd left a string of 401(k) money at old companies, had too much just sitting in a savings account, and had no clue how much he had or where it was. There was a feeling of dread that all this was about to catch up with him, or one day people who admired him would find out what a loser he was with money. His daydream? Literally getting a visual dashboard that showed where all his money was and how it was performing once a quarter . . . and then never having to deal with it.

This became the basis for this advisor's offering of full-stewardship financial management for high-earning people who wanted to build wealth and live a comfortable lifestyle now.

For my own clients, the Pit of Despair is all about the feeling that they're just spinning their wheels on social media, posting random nonsense that isn't doing their business any good. They're afraid to be absent from the space but are sure they don't know enough about how to use digital content to drive meaningful results. The worst part is, they don't know what they don't know! With all the deep expertise these clients hold, it drives them to distraction not to be able to master something they think should be much simpler, like social media and digital content. They have a sinking feeling that their business will fail because they can't figure this one thing out.

The language you develop while hanging out in the Pit of Despair with your Best. Client. Ever! is problem language, not solution language. It's the words they use to describe the 7-layer crap salad in which they find themselves. Once you feel like you have a full handle on the problem, let's think about what life looks like once they get out of the Pit of Despair with you.

- What does life look like with this problem solved? How does your client feel? How is she sleeping?

- What emotions does she no longer have to carry?

- What can she do now as a result of having that problem solved?

- What can she be proud of?

Our example advisor knew this would take so much shame and uncertainty off his clients' plates. His clients would never have to worry about being seen as a loser. They'd have it together when it came to money, and that meant they'd finally dealt with their most important loose ends. They'd be free to really enjoy what they were building, with a feeling of relief and freedom.

The language that comes out of these questions is your solution language. Those big, gorgeous FEELING words that express the feeling your clients so desperately desire, is the feeling you're offering when they work with you to achieve transformation.

A WORD OF WARNING: We're about to dive into search data. Typically, your Best. Client. Ever! will use their problem language when searching—not the solution language. This isn't always the case, but it's a good rule of thumb when starting out.

✍ BEST. CLIENT. EVER!

- **DEMOGRAPHICS**
  (Only answer the ones that are relevant to your ideal client)

  - Gender: . . . .
  - Age: . . . .
  - Geography: . . . .
  - Education: . . . .
  - Income: . . . .
  - Occupation: . . . .
  - Marital Status: . . . .
  - Parental Status: . . . .

  Photo of your
  Best. Client. Ever!

- **EXPLAIN LIFE CIRCUMSTANCES**
  (for example: Divorce, new business, professional dissatisfaction, health issues, crisis of purpose)

- At her lowest moment, what is your Best. Client. Ever! struggling with?

- What does she daydream about? What does her fantasy look like if her most pressing problem was solved?

- What does she feel guilty about?

- What does she worry she's not good enough to do?

- What's the life goal she's afraid to tell everyone?

- What's the transformation she needs?

Leveraging Search Data

What an amazing time to be alive as a content creator! I'm serious. We have so many fantastic tools at our disposal to determine what our audiences care about—there's no excuse for writing content that's not relevant to them. Thanks to the ubiquity of Google and Bing searches, we can see clearly what people are searching for, what content they're finding most valuable, and even how they're wording their questions. Here are some of my favorite tools for using search data to get to know my Best. Client. Ever!

AnswerThePublic.com

This web-based tool is the bee's knees when it comes to generating content ideas. Simply type in your general key phrase (remember, look at that problem language your prospect is experiencing!) and it will provide you with a series of visual mind maps that show you the most common search queries associated with that search term.

More than anything, AnswerThePublic.com gives you new ways to view what your client is searching for. For example, I was working with an Equine Therapist who had no idea that so many people were wondering how they could PAY for equine therapy services. There were a host of questions about insurance and Medicaid, and how much the services cost. That led her to create an entire content series on the topic, bringing her traffic like she'd never seen before.

AnswerThePublic.com has a free version that allows you to search a few search terms per day. I've been advised, however, to let you know about the intense biz bro that makes super creepy too-long eye contact with you when you arrive at AnswerThePublic.com. You've been warned.

SEMRush

SEMRush is a similar tool, but it provides you with two important pieces of data—monthly search volume and the competition score. The higher the competition score is, the harder it is to rank for it on the search engine results page (SERP). The unicorn here, of course, is finding a search term with high monthly volume and low competition.

The Keyword Magic Tool within SEMRush will give you recommendations for related search terms along with the search volume and competition.

SEMRush offers a 14-day free trial.

BuzzSumo

Using BuzzSumo, you can key in a search term you want to rank for, and it will show you the content that searchers have found most useful for that search term. From there, look at what those "most useful" sites have created. Where can you fill in holes? Create something richer and more interesting? How can you create something even better and more useful?

BuzzSumo allows you a few free searches per day.

Your keyword sweet spot

As you're using these tools to figure out your keywords, one of the challenge is figuring out how all these numbers work together. Keyword competition? Search volume? What's most important?

Your ideal keywords will be highly aligned to your brand, expertise and offering. The more relevant they are to what you do, the higher quality the traffic you get will be. Your best keywords will also have a lower competition score, meaning fewer others are trying to rank for them, and moderate search volume.

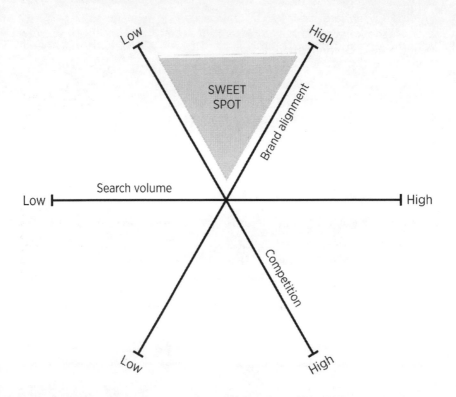

✍ Keyword Ideas

As you're using AnswerThePublic.com and SEMRush, you'll be developing your initial topic ideas for your Content Goldmine. Make note of the keywords/terms and topics that seem to be of most interest.

How do the search volume and competition numbers look? More importantly, where does each keyword align with your offering and brand? The keyword that works best for you will be the one you build your Content Goldmine around.

Keyword ideas	Volume?	Competition?	Brand alignment?

I Spy

At this point, we've done about as much as we can to get to know your Best. Client. Ever! without going straight to the source. For this, I'm a firm believer in good old-fashioned spying.

And again, for someone trying to build a business, there's never been a better time to conduct marketing research. The first place to start is in Facebook Groups. Find three to five groups who serve a similar audience to yours . . . And start spying. What are they talking about? What are they worried about? What are they engaging most with? What are they responding to? What are they fighting about?

Within most of these groups, you can even ask questions. What's your biggest struggle when it comes to X? What's your ultimate goal when it comes to X? If you could solve one problem when it comes to X, what would it be?

Or even better, you can test small messages by crafting a short post giving advice or information. It takes just a few minutes, and you can use the resulting engagement as a barometer of the interest of the audience in the topic.

Other places to spy include subreddits on your topic or Instagram hashtags related to your topic. Whichever platform you feel most comfortable on is where you should conduct your audience research.

Asking

When you have a question, the best thing you can do is ask, right? If you already have clients, why not directly ask them why they chose you? What was the main problem they wanted help with? Why you and not someone else? The answer you get may surprise you and inform your direction for finding new clients.

You can do this in the form of a survey, using Survey Monkey or Typeform. Or you can simply do this one-on-one at the end of a coaching engagement or part of your regular intake. You already have access to your clients. Why not take a moment to find out what it was about you that attracted them?

Competitive Research

An indirect (but powerful) way to work through what your clients need is to look at what your competitors are doing. What are they offering? What's their unique angle? What's their unique voice and personality? What kind of content are they providing?

The added benefit for doing some solid competitor research upfront is that it lets you know where there is any "white space"—an area that competitors are not covering that is meaningful to your client.

To start your competitive research, begin with your top 3–4 known competitors. Google the companies and make note of what you see in terms of offerings, tone and voice, content, and positioning (we'll discuss more on these concepts in Chapter 3). Do the same for UNKNOWN competitors. Google your category and select up to 3 that you didn't know about before and perform the same analysis. Can you see how each competitor is somewhat different from one another? What works and what doesn't? What's missing from the ecosystem?

Check out SEMRush for competitive research. Enter your competitor's web address in the Domain Insights tool, and it will tell you what keywords that site ranks for, show you the competitor's paid search engine ads, and landing pages. It's an extremely helpful way to get your arms around the content ecosystem and messaging of your main competitors.

NOTE: Competitor research can turn into a raging time suck. You can lose yourself in it forever if you're not careful. I strongly recommend only looking at 3–4 known competitors and up to 3 new competitors within about 90 minutes. From there, take what you know and walk The. Hell. Away! Time to play your own game.

✒ Competitive Analysis

Use the table below as a place to record observations about 3-6 competitors. You should already have at least 3 competitors in mind—experts in your area who are more well-known and established with your ideal audience than you are. The remaining 2-3 competitors are businesses you may not be aware of yet and discover via search.

Competitor	How does the offering compare to yours?	Content focus	Tone and personality	Primary audience

- How is your offering different from your competitors?

- How can your content be DIFFERENT from competitors?

- How is your brand voice and personality different?

- What makes your Best. Client. Ever! different from who your competitors are targeting?

- What are none of these competitors doing, saying, or being that you can do, say, or be?

CHAPTER 2 - **SUMMARY**

- *Go three layers deep to get specific about your target audience.*

- *Spend some time in the Pit of Despair with your client to reconnect with the problem they most want to solve and the language they use around it.*

- *Use tools like AnswerThePublic.com, SEMRush and BuzzSumo to see what people are really searching for.*

- *Spy on your Best. Client. Ever! in Facebook Groups, subReddits and Instagram hashtags.*

- *Ask your clients why they chose you.*

- *Spend no more than 90 minutes on competitive research to see what else is available to clients in terms of offering, content, angle and brand voice.*

NOTES

CHAPTER 3:

Real Deal Brand Building Blocks

Coco Chanel said it best:

> *In order to be irreplaceable,*
> *one must always be different.*

And your level of expertise should garner you irreplaceable status with the people you serve. In order for them to view you in that way, you need to package that expertise in a way that meets their unique needs, stands out from the sea of competitors, and makes it clear that who you are aligns with your Best. Client. Ever! Building your unique personal brand as an expert, coach, or consultant is the foundational work of getting known for what you do best.

Why brand matters

In the world of corporate marketing and advertising agencies, when someone is discussing "brand consistency" or "brand strength," they're talking about how *visually* recognizable a brand is. And while a logo is an important component of a corporate brand, in the world of expert, coach and consulting brands, it's not a first priority. In fact, a logo is something you can address pretty quickly and inexpensively.

I have a lot of graphic design and brand strategist friends who would disagree with me on this, but I'll say it anyway: a great logo is easy to come by. But for an expert, coach, or consultant who wants to be known, the most important elements of the brand come in the form of *your unique and consistently applied message and authentic voice.*

When you're building a business that's all about who you are and what you offer, a well-defined and consistently applied message is a highly practical commodity. It sets you apart from your competitors, speaks in a resonant way to your Best. Client. Ever! and creates an expectation of what kind of content you'll produce to help your target audience.

In the last chapter, you laid out your Best. Client. Ever! Keep that information front and center as you're working through your brand message and voice. Understanding the pain and goals of your Best. Client. Ever! is foundational to creating a message that's relevant, gets attention, and drives profitable customer action. After all, you can't build a message that connects with people until you know what people need, right?

The structure of your unique brand message

I like to think of the personal brand message strategy of an expert, coach or consultant as a house. There are certain components that are needed to make it stand at all and in fact, truly be a house (foundation, walls, a roof). And then there are the elements that make the house attractive to passersby. Imagine that this is your brand house.

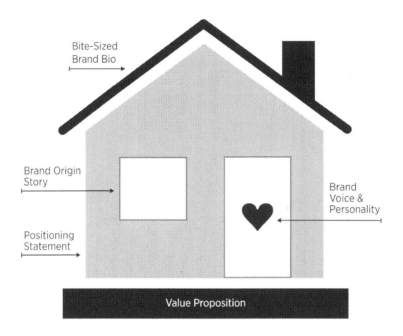

Within the house, there are 6 critical elements to nail down in order for you to have a functioning brand that communicates what you're about, attracts the right people, and tells the wrong people to keep on walking.

Value Proposition = The Foundation

Just as a solid foundation is what makes a house stand straight and not sink into the ground, your Value Proposition is what makes you a legitimate service provider with something to offer. The Value Proposition is a tool for you to define your offering, what problem it solves, and what evidence you have that you can deliver.

Positioning Statement = The Frame and Walls

The frame and walls of a house are what make one house look different from another. It gives your brand house a different shape. Even if your Value Proposition is the same or similar to others, you can use your Positioning to make it your own— whether that means appealing to a different audience, standing against conventional wisdom, or completely rewriting the script of the category. The Positioning is what makes people see you.

Brand Voice & Personality = The Decor

This is what gives your brand curb appeal. It's what makes a potential client look at you and say "I like that. That really looks like a house that I could fall in love with." The goal is to translate your Value Proposition and Positioning Statement through the lens of your unique voice and personality so passersby say, "Yup, that's something I really like, and that feels like home."

Brand Origin Story = The Doors and Windows

Your Brand Origin Story is the doors and windows of your house. This is how people get inside. It's the part of your brand that pulls people in and lets them know that it's safe to be in this house, and that it's a comfortable place to be where they'll find people like them. It's the part of your brand that lets them feel that they know you because you're sharing your "why" and connecting with them—human to human.

Content Mission Statement = Floor Plan

While you're probably familiar with an organizational Mission Statement (clearly outlines the mission of the organization is), your Content Mission Statement is more specific. It tells prospects exactly what the content you produce will help them to accomplish. It's like a house's floor plan – it tells you exactly what you can do in this home, what to expect once they come inside, and the functions they'll be able to accomplish.

Bite-Sized Brand Bio = The Roof from 5,000 Feet Up

When your Best. Client. Ever! is flying over at 5,000 feet—seeing hundreds of seemingly identical houses—your Bite-Sized Brand Bio is the only thing that can tell her you're somehow different. Maybe your roof is green instead of grey. Maybe your Bite-Sized Brand Bio in a sea of experts and coaches on social media tells her that you work specifically with people in a certain age group, or have a dark sense of humor, or think manifestation is a joke. It's your place to QUICKLY align with her on a commonality, so she knows you're meant for her.

Your Value Proposition

There are literally a million formulas out there for creating an effective Value Proposition. Some are more useful than others, but none of them are geared toward the personal brands that experts, coaches, consultants, advisors and professional service providers need to build in order to create a loyal client base and following. So what I've developed is the 3 Ps: Problem, Product, and Proof.

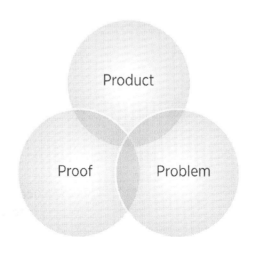

The problem is easy. We covered that in the previous chapter. This is what your Best. Client. Ever! is desperate to solve, what's keeping them up at night, and what you're uniquely qualified to solve for them.

The product? That's you.

Well, you and your offering. Your coaching packages, courses, membership offering, training services, and the like. As we think through each component of your offering, we'll notice three categories: Table stakes, differentiators, and game changers.

- **Table stakes:** These are the things you offer or attributes of your business that are just the cost of entry. If you're a life coach, you need to be a certified coach and offer coaching packages. Otherwise, you're not a life coach. If you're a mental health professional, you need your LMHP, and you need to offer counseling sessions. If you're a personal trainer, you need to offer personal training. If you're a financial advisor, you should have a CFP and you offer investment advice. Nothing unique about any of this, but this is all required in order to BE the kind of expert you claim to be.

- **Differentiators:** These are exactly what they sound like . . . services or qualifications that are different—either on their face or because of how they're packaged. Maybe in addition to your table stakes offering as a life coach, you use a certain type of assessment or follow a particular philosophy that not everyone uses. Or as a business strategist, you have certain qualifications—like a HubSpot Academy certification or a Google Search certification, and maybe you adhere to a certain expert's approach and are endorsed by that experts. As a graphic designer, perhaps you have a package for startup businesses where you give them a basic branding package, along with some on-going retainer work. These are NOT groundbreaking offerings, but qualifications that not EVERYONE has, or service offerings that not EVERYONE does. Your differentiator could also be a specific area of expertise—maybe you only work with health care professionals or women who have just been divorced or widowed. Or maybe your differentiator is a specific philosophical alignment—biblically-based investing, or environmentally sustainable business practices.

- **Game changers:** These are the things you offer that you believe are so unique and so relevant to your audience that they have the potential to be your signature offering. For that life coach from above, maybe she's focused on pushing people out of their comfort zones so they can live braver lives. Maybe she offers a weekend Brave Adventure getaway with a high-ropes course, fire walking, polar plunges and a host of other experiences designed to make you uncomfortable AND show you what overcoming that discomfort feels like. Maybe that business strategist we talked about offers a virtual matchmaking event to pair up start-ups with other start-ups that offer services that they need, who all follow the same philosophy. Or maybe it's just your particular framework—something that you can brand and make your own. Like the Marie Kondo's Konmari Method. Or Brene Brown's BRAVING Framework for the seven elements of trust. You don't have to be famous to have your own framework. Doing so gives people a way to understand what it is you do.

- If you're looking at the last category and fretting because you don't have a game changer yet, don't worry. Typically, you find your game changer the more you learn about and interact with your Best. Client. Ever! As you get deeper into what they really need and see what content they essentially respond to, you'll identify Game Changer opportunities.

- To get a clear view of your Product within the Value Proposition, start by inventorying your existing offering. What components are Table Stakes? Which are Differentiators? Do you already have an idea or two for a Game Changer offering?

- Once you have a clear idea of how much of your offering is Table Stakes vs. Differentiator or Game Changer, you know where you need to put some work in. If you have no Differentiating elements in your offering, for example, it's time to do some thinking on that. What does your Best. Client. Ever! need that you can offer above and beyond your Table Stakes?

Use this inventory sheet to list out your product elements:

✍ Value Proposition Inventory

TABLE STAKES	DIFFERENTIATORS	GAME CHANGERS
What do you offer that's just plain ordinary? You have to offer it in order to be considered legit.	What's something that makes you stand out? Others may have it, but definitely not everyone.	What are your BIG differences? The things that have the potential to make you totally unique?

The proof. Show us the evidence.

The last P in your Value Proposition is the Proof. This is the hurdle that you must overcome in order to show that you really CAN solve the problem. Proof comes in the form of testimonials from past clients, certifications and degrees (these are table stakes in some cases, but also act as proof of your qualifications and ability to do the work), specific areas of training, statistics that say a certain approach you use does work or a guarantee. The proof is what makes the user feel safe spending time and money with you.

Creating Your Value Proposition

Now that we have a clearer idea of the Product, Problem and Proof, let's build out your complete Value Proposition. The Value Proposition lives where the PROBLEM your audiences are having overlaps with the PRODUCT you offer, and the PROOF that you can solve this problem. Let's break down what each of these is.

The PROBLEM is a real, pressing situation in the life of your Best. Client. Ever! It's something that's continually pushing in on them, that needs to be solved. In your world, this could be the hard-driving career mom's new and continual dissatisfaction with work and the knowledge that there is SOMETHING more for her . . . she just doesn't know how to even go about trying to figure that out. Or the problem is past trauma tanking present relationships. Or persistent symptoms that traditional medicine hasn't solved. Or the problem is being unable to afford a personal trainer but being unable to figure out how to effectively lose weight without one.

That's where the PRODUCT comes in. And the product is what you offer. It's your solution to that problem. It's a coaching package, or a course, or a book, or a group membership—and there's part or all of that offering that's a perfect solution for the audience's problem. The PROOF swoops in and reinforces what you say is true.

Use this sheet to create your Value Proposition:

✍ Write Your Value Proposition

- The problem I solve is:

- The solution I offer is:

- You know it's true because of:

  > **Proof point 1:** ....
  >
  > **Proof point 2:** ....
  >
  > **Proof point 3:** ....

For example, if I'm a Habit Coach for work-from-home professionals, I might say, the problem I solve is: Professionals are making terrible use of their WFH time, resulting in dissatisfaction, depression and a feeling of failure.

The solution I offer is: My Optimal Habit coaching package.

The results I create are: Greater productivity, more balance, and more control over your life.

You know it's true because of:

- My coaching credentials
- My experience in Productivity Consulting for Fortune 500s
- This thorough eBook I wrote on the topic
- The testimonial from this client

Or if I'm a therapist specializing in eating disorders, I might have this:

The problem I solve is: Eating disorders.

The solution I offer is: My specialized eye-movement desensitization approach.

The results I create are: More control over disordered eating behaviors.

You know it's true because of:

- Years of experience in specialization
- Endorsements from a society
- My appearances in the media

So you'll notice that your Value Proposition is inherently fact-based. Its purpose is to serve as a guidepost for you as you build your business. When you think about branching out and creating new offerings, you can ask yourself—does this offering adhere to the Value Proposition? And as we get further in the book and the questions become:

- Does this content support the Value Proposition?

- Does it add another proof point?

- Does it show the results?

- Does it teach the solution?

- Does it illuminate the problem?

Before moving on to the next section, please take some time to work on your fact-based Value Proposition, and outline your offering using the sheet provided.

Positioning Statement

While your Value Proposition was all facts about YOU, your Positioning Statement is all about *context*—where you fit in the mind of the consumer. The purpose of a Positioning Statement is to frame how you show up to your ideal client with your offering, and what you're best at relative to the rest of your category— other experts, coaches and consultants serving the same audience.

Remember how we talked about how it was the framing of the house? This is how you want your Best. Client. Ever! to see you compared to others in your category.

The formula for your Positioning Statement is:

WHAT: The only [category]
HOW: that [differentiating characteristic]
WHO: for [your best client ever]
WHY: who [need state]
WHEN: during [underlying trend].

Here's an example from an iconic American brand, Harley Davidson. This is their actual Positioning Statement:

WHAT: The only motorcycle manufacturer
HOW: that makes big, loud motorcycles

WHO: for macho guys (and "macho wannabes")
mostly in the United States
WHY: who want to join a gang of cowboys
WHEN: during an era of decreasing personal freedom.

Here's Ikea's Positioning Statement:

WHAT: The only home furnishing store
HOW: that creates stylish, affordable furniture
WHO: for Starving Artist Sarah
WHY: who wants a well-designed home
WHEN: while everything else in life is getting more expensive.

So how do we translate that to the personal brand of an expert, coach or consultant who serves a specific audience? Take a look at these:

WHAT: The only marketing coach
HOW: that offers actionable, straight-talk strategies
WHO: to start-up solo coaches, counselors and experts
WHY: who want to use digital content to build their businesses, but don't know how
WHEN: in an environment where fluffy, platitude-pushing gurus are a dime a dozen, and technology keeps getting more complex.

WHAT: The only health and fitness coach
HOW: that offer gentle, fun, doable approaches
WHO: to those 55+ and extremely overweight
WHY: who need to lose weight on doctor's orders
WHEN: without becoming a fitness nut or leaving their comfort foods behind.

WHAT: The only Registered Investment Advisor
HOW: who provides total financial management
WHO: to millennials who don't want to deal with it
WHY: but want to build wealth without thinking about it
WHEN: in a world where it's too easy to lose money as soon as it comes in.

Your Positioning Statement and Value Proposition are for you. These aren't externally facing.

Rather they act as the foundational elements for how you'll create the other elements of your brand AND as a checklist for your content.

For every piece of content you consider creating, you'll have your Value Proposition to hold them up against, to ask if this content is true to those foundational elements.

Build out your Positioning Statement now:

You are the only ....
(service category)

that ....
(unique offering/characteristic)

for ....
(Your Best. Client. Ever!)

Who ....
(state of need, desire or pain)

During ....
(underlying trend)

Brand Voice & Personality

For some reason I don't understand, brand voice is a tough one for solo experts, coaches and consultants to nail down. Either they come from a clinical background and are afraid to let loose, they're from a corporate background, and can't release their hyperbizjargonizing, or they don't want to commit to a tone of voice that might alienate people.

My advice is this: Alienate people. You want to.

It's true. Your Brand Voice & Personality are the flower boxes in your brand house. It's the curb appeal that attracts the right people. But it also needs to repel the wrong people. Think "repel" is too strong a word? It's not. Your Brand Voice & Personality should tell the wrong people to keep on freaking walking. Nothing here for you . . .

Why? Because working with the wrong people is joyless. If your Brand Voice & Personality is all about fun and irreverence, you do not want to work with people who take everything too seriously and get easily offended.

If your brand is all about gentleness and compassion, you do not want to work with hyper-aggressive beast-moders.

If your brand is all about self-empowerment and personal accountability, you do not want to work with perpetual victims.

Your Brand Voice & Personality is one of the most powerful tools in your arsenal to make sure the right people are landing in your inbox and the wrong people are staying the hell away.

With that out of the way, let's talk about what Brand Voice & Personality is. Brand Voice & Personality is your commitment to a set of attributes that permeates your content, creating a consistent emotional experience for people. You build out your set of attributes to dictate how your content feels and sounds and how it does NOT feel and sound.

Now, the first mistake people make with this exercise is getting WAY too aspirational. You want to articulate a brand voice and personality that expresses who you ARE, not who you think you should be.

Can who you are be expressed in a few adjectives? Of course not, you're far too complicated. What I do want you to think about is a few parts of your personality that have served you best when it comes to connecting with people. For me, I'm extremely casual, kind of nerdy, and I make people laugh. So that is what I built my brand personality around. Other parts of my personality? I also have a short temper, hold a grudge like no-one's business, swear at really inappropriate times. I opted NOT to build my brand voice and personality around those little quirks.

I advise starting with 4–6 core attributes that resonate most strongly with you. From there, dive deep and define what each of these means to you. When you're done creating your Brand Voice & Personality, you'll have a powerful checklist for every piece of content that you write.

Put simply: If your Value Proposition is what you say, then your Brand Voice & Personality is how you say it.

Start with this list of attributes and circle the ones that speak most strongly to you. Narrow it down and combine them to reach 4–6 primary attributes. From there, move to the Brand Voice & Positioning Worksheet on the following page.

Potential Brand Attributes

Able	Easy-going	Insightful	Persistent
Active	Empathetic	Intelligent	Pleasant
Adaptable	Enduring	Interesting	Positive
Adventurous	Energetic	Intuitive	Practical
Ambitious	Enterprising	Inventive	Principled
Authentic	Enthusiastic	Jolly	Quick-witted
Aware	Ethical	Jovial	Rational
Balanced	Excited	Joyful	Real
Bold	Exuberant	Kind	Reasonable
Brave	Fair	Knowledgeable	Reflective
Calm	Fascinating	Laid-back	Reliable
Capable	Feisty	Light-hearted	Resilient
Carefree	Fervent	Likeable	Resourceful
Caring	Flexible	Lively	Respectful
Cheerful	Friendly	Loveable	Responsible
Clever	Fun	Loyal	Sensitive
Compassionate	Generous	Magical	Sharp
Confident	Gentle	Mature	Sincere
Conscientious	Genuine	Memorable	Smart
Considerate	Giving	Motivated	Spirited
Courageous	Gutsy	Natural	Spiritual
Creative	Happy	Neat	Spontaneous
Curious	Hardworking	Noble	Stable
Dainty	Healthy	Nurturing	Steady
Daring	Helpful	Observant	Strong
Dedicated	Honest	Open-minded	Studious
Dependable	Honorable	Optimistic	Supportive
Determined	Humble	Organized	Surprising
Devoted	Humorous	Original	Thorough
Diligent	Idealistic	Outgoing	Thoughtful
Direct	Imaginative	Patient	Tireless
Disciplined	Independent	Patriotic	Trustworthy
Dynamic	Ingenius	Peaceful	Upbeat
Eager	Inquisitive	Perceptive	Warm

✍ Your Brand Voice & Personality

List your 5 attributes here:

Attribute 1

....

What does this mean to you?

....

What does his NOT mean?

....

Attribute 2

....

What does this mean to you?

....

What does his NOT mean?

....

Attribute 3

....

What does this mean to you?

....

What does his NOT mean?

....

Attribute 4

....

What does this mean to you?

....

What does his NOT mean?

....

Attribute 5

....

What does this mean to you?

....

What does his NOT mean?

....

Brand Origin Story

Let's dive into the meatiest one of all your foundational brand content—the Brand Origin Story. If you'll think back to our house diagram at the beginning of the chapter, you'll remember that the Brand Origin Story is your doors and windows. This is what lets people see inside your brand to the person within. It's a powerful way for your Best. Client. Ever! to understand you and feel like they can relate to your story, making it easier for them to trust you with their business.

The diagram below is something you may have seen in writing classes or even in regards to brand storytelling. It's a diagram of the Hero's Journey, which is Joseph Campbell's mythic storytelling structure. You'll see this structure in so many of our most beloved stories—from Star Wars to Lord of the Rings to Harry Potter to Captain America to Guardians of the Galaxy to Bridget Jones's Diary. It is everywhere. And it's everywhere because it's a story structure that humans have been telling and hearing for centuries so that we are hard-wired to understand it.

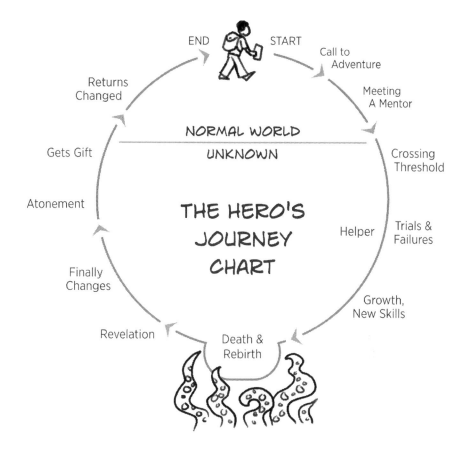

If we look at the diagram, the hero starts in the normal world. Things are going along just fine and dandy until something happens that necessitates the hero to leave the normal world to solve a problem. This is the **Call to Adventure.** Shortly thereafter the hero **Meets a Mentor**—Obi-Wan Kenobi, Gandolf, Hagrid— the guide who is going to teach the hero what they need to know to solve the problem, and help them as they move into the unknown.

That first step into the unknown is **Crossing the Threshold.** From there, our hero undergoes **Trials and Failures** and gains **New Skills and Growth** until they run into a challenge they cannot overcome.

The setback, called **Death & Rebirth** is catastrophic, and it has the potential to derail the journey entirely. This transformative moment leads to a great **Revelation** that puts the hero back on her path with renewed purpose. She's able to make the **Changes**—usually to mindset—to push through and finally make things right through **Atonement.** The hero is then rewarded (**Gets Gift**), and **Returns Changed** to the normal world.

I always think of the end of Harry Potter and the Sorcerer's Stone (the movie, not the book) as the perfect example of Returning Changed.

> "It feels strange to be going home, doesn't it?"
> asks Hermione.
>
> "I'm not going home. Not really,"
> answers Harry.

He's hopping on the Hogwarts Express, heading back to the normal world. But he's changed, Hogwarts has become the place where he belongs, and Number 4 Privet Drive will never be home again.

Let's take a look at how the Hero's Journey can help us build a brand origin story that applies to your own personal brand as a coach, consultant or expert service provider.

Example: A Nonprofit Strategy Coach

- **The Call to Adventure:** I was living an ordinary life in an ordinary corporate job. The money was good, the benefits were great. But I couldn't shake the feeling that I was meant for something more. I just didn't know what . . . until a volunteer opportunity arose to facilitate strategic planning with a local nonprofit.

- **Meeting a Mentor:** As I worked with the nonprofit, it occurred to me that they were crippling their impact by being so disorganized. I had spent the last 20 years organizing teams around a common goal, and helping them develop strategies that got the job done. I could have a serious impact working with nonprofits. But was this even a real *thing* that people needed? I did some research and found Jane Martinelli. While I had two decades of successful corporate strategy experience, I didn't quite know how to translate that to a nonprofit setting. Jane had many of the same skills as me, but had built her career on helping nonprofits get their ducks in a row.

- **Crossing the Threshold:** So, I booked an hour with Jane and learned how she got started. That was it for me. I was past the point of no return now. This was no longer just a one-off volunteer appointment. I knew that I could help this nonprofit (and countless others) get out of their own way and maximize their work. And getting some insight from Jane on how to get started right was exactly what I needed. I reached out to my nonprofit connections and started working with some of them immediately on their strategic plans and long-term visions.

- **Trials & Failures:** But as I worked with more and more nonprofits, I saw that over and over again the strategies that I recommended were not being implemented. Aside from the exercise of my strategic planning framework, they were getting nothing from working with me.

- **Growth & New Skills:** The framework must be flawed, I reasoned. So I undertook an exhaustive study of successful, high-impact nonprofits and their strategic planning process. Soon, I had uncovered 10 clear-cut, absolute differences between how high-performing nonprofits and mediocre ones did their planning.

- **Death & Rebirth:** So I put the 10 differences into action. This was a framework that should have changed everything . . . but it didn't. It changed nothing. For anyone. I lost clients. People stopped calling me. And I sank into a depression. I almost gave up. My husband recommended that I talk with a coach.

- **Revelation:** The time with the coach was NOT what I expected. I went seeking for strategies. What I got was mindset talk. At first, I was annoyed. But after some of the mindset work started to take hold within me, it hit me like a bolt of lightning: THE FRAMEWORK WASN'T WRONG. But if the organizational mindset is wrong, the framework was irrelevant. Unless I addressed organizational mindset issues upfront, no framework would ever take hold.

- **Finally Changes:** I called an old nonprofit friend and said I'd work for free. Just let me try this one thing! For the first three sessions, we dove deep into the mindset issues of the organization, learning that the nonprofit employees (even leadership!) felt that strategic planning was at best a waste of time, and at worst a problematic distraction from their direct service work.

- **Atonement:** After the mindset work with the team, they were actually able to internalize and implement the framework. And the changes stuck! I was able to bring this new revelation to some of the clients I had previously failed and helped them create real change in their organizations.

- **Gets Gift:** One of my most transformed clients nominated me as the keynote speaker for the region's largest nonprofit conference. The event allowed me to share the message with 500+ organizations . . . and earned me a nice new stack of clients!

- **Returns Changed:** Now, nonprofit consulting is my full-time gig. I work when I want to, travel more, and have a burning passion for the organizations that I serve. There is nothing in the world like doing what you know you are meant to do. I think back to my ho-hum corporate job, and can't even imagine myself in that spot.

How to use the Brand Origin Story

Once you create your Brand Origin Story, you can use it in multiple ways:

- As the About page on your website

- As your speaker bio

- As your About the Author section in an eBook or other long-form content piece

- Repurposed into multiple long-form social media posts or blog posts.

The structure presented here can be used for more stories than just yours. Imagine using this for client stories, or even an imaginary Best. Client. Ever! The Hero's Journey structure can paint an emotional picture of how your services can transform people. Use the client stories as case studies, blog posts, long-form social media posts, or anecdotes in your presentations. You'll hear it from me a lot—repurposing is the name of the game.

✍ Your Brand Origin Story

- Your call to adventure...

  ....

  ....

- Meeting a mentor...

  ....

  ....

- Crossing a threshold...

  ....

  ....

- Trials & Failures...

  ....

  ....

✍ Your Brand Origin Story

- Your call to adventure…

  ....
  ....

- Meeting a mentor…

  ....
  ....

- Crossing a threshold…

  ....
  ....

- Trials & Failures…

  ....
  ....

- Growth, New Skills

  ....
  ....

- Death & Rebirth

  ....
  ....

- Revelation

  ....

  ....

- Finally Changes

  ....

  ....

- Atonement

  ....

  ....

- Gets Gift

  ....

  ....

- Returns Changed

  ....

  ....

- The End!

  ....

  ....

Once you understand the structure of a Brand Origin Story, you'll start seeing it everywhere there's a beloved brand. Apple's origin story is standing up to the artless, soulless and overly complex interfaces of the first personal computing devices to create simple, functional, beautiful technology.

Tony Robbins' Brand Origin Story is about wanting to help people NOW, but the psychiatric establishment was moving too slowly, so he became the breakout hero.

Dyson vacuums came about because of James Dyson's frustration with vacuums that lost suction and his obsessive, super-nerdy quest to figure out why.

Frequently, the community built around a brand is proportionate to the strength of the Brand Origin Story.

Content Mission Statement

Alright, now that you've completed your Brand Origin Story, let's dive into the Content Mission Statement so that your Best. Client. Ever! knows just what kind of learning they can expect from your content. This will help them make the choice to join your Facebook group, subscribe to emails, read your blog, or find other ways to become involved in your content ecosystem.

First, let's clearly define what a Content Mission Statement is:

> CONTENT MISSION STATEMENT: Declaration of intent for your content. A clear breakdown of what users can expect to learn from you consistently and how it will help them.

ALSO: It's the best focusing tool you'll ever have for determining what kind of content to create for the short and long term. As soon as you get an idea for a piece of content, you can immediately come back to your Content Mission Statement. If an idea doesn't fit within that statement, you should not be wasting your time with it. Period.

3 Essential elements of a Content Mission Statement

Your Content Mission Statement is not something you want to complicate. Its focusing power comes from its simplicity. Your Content Mission Statement has 3 essential elements:

1. Identification of your core audience.

2. What will be delivered for that audience?

3. The ultimate outcome for that audience.

And that's it!

INC. Magazine, for example, has this as their Content Mission Statement:

> *Welcome to INC.com, the place where entrepreneurs and business owners can find useful information, advice, insights, resources and inspiration for running and growing their businesses.*

Pretty clear, right? The identified audience is entrepreneurs and business owners. What will be delivered is useful information, advice, insights, resources and inspiration. And the ultimate outcome for the audience is to grow their businesses.

Let's look at HomeMadeSimple.com. They also have a clear, concise Content Mission Statement that follows the same approach:

> *Whether it's a delicious recipe, an inspiring décor idea, or a refreshing approach to organizing, we strive to help on-the-go moms create a home that's truly your own.*

The identified audience? On-the-go moms. The content that will be delivered? Recipes, décor ideas and organizing tips. The ultimate outcome the site is helping the audience achieve? Creating a home that truly feels like her.

The Orbiter blog focuses on digital marketing best practices. They take the same approach to their Content Mission Statement:

> *The Orbiter blog is where digital marketers find expert, practical advice on web design and content marketing. Our goal is to help you get better results from the web.*

The identified audience? Digital marketers. The content delivered? Expert, practical advice on web design and content marketing. The ultimate outcome? The audience gets better results from the web.

You get the idea. Now, with a clear idea of your Best. Client. Ever! and what they care about, your Value Proposition and Brand Positioning, you have everything you need to create your Content Mission Statement.

....

....

....

....

....

....

....

....

....

Using your Content Mission Statement

Unlike your Positioning Statement, your Content Mission Statement is absolutely public. This is a declaration and promise that you're making to your users, and you should make it visible in the right places, including:

- As part of your blog's masthead (and as the search description for your blog page)

- Your header image on your YouTube channel

- At the bottom of each blog post

- In a prominent spot on your email newsletter

- On the sign-up page for your email newsletter

- At the beginning of each podcast episode

- To kickoff your webinars

And don't worry, you don't have to get clever with your Content Mission Statement for each place you use it. This is an instance where repetition will do you good. Copy. Paste. Move on!

Bite-Sized Brand Bio

If you think back to the beginning of the chapter, I compared the Bite-Sized Brand Bio to a big, highly visible label on the roof of your brand house. It's so that a user flying over in a helicopter at 5,000 feet—looking down at all the potential experts, coaches and consultants available—will be able to spot your brand and determine at a glance if you warrant consideration.

So what is a Bite-Sized Brand Bio? It's an itty-bitty, snackable piece of content that totally encapsulates YOU and what you're about. And you use it just about everywhere.

Your Bite-Sized Brand Bio describes your offering (in words) and your personality (in voice and tone). It qualifies your Best. Client. Ever! by speaking directly to their most critical needs. And most importantly, it *disqualifies* clients who wouldn't be a good fit by clearly showing your personality and setting expectations of what problem you'll solve. If that problem isn't their problem? They can just keep on walking . . .

So how small is bite-sized, you may ask? Real small, 150–175 characters, give or take. Before you start panicking, let's take a look at the formula for creating a Bite-Sized Brand Bio as well as some examples.

Bite-Sized Brand Bio Formula

MY (unique adjective) + (product or service)
+ (thing your customer will be able to do)
SO YOU CAN (how it will change client's life)

Let's say that the Therapist we talked about before who specializes in eating disorders wants to write her Bite-Sized Brand Bio. The approach she uses is called Eye Movement Desensitization Therapy, and it's a unique approach for her particular audience and the problem they're trying to solve. So her Bite-Sized Brand Bio might look like this:

My proven Eye Movement Desensitization Therapy
helps eating disorder patients like you take control
of your thoughts
so you can finally rebuild a healthy life!

Does it describe? Yes, she's a therapist who uses EMD for eating disorder patients.

Does it qualify? Yes, it's for eating disorder patients.

Does it disqualify? Yes, if you're not an eating disorder patient, this isn't for you.

Now let's look at the Executive Coach we've talked about. Her Bite-Sized Brand Bio might look like this:

My High-Performer Portfolio approach
places 100% of clients at goal salary or higher
so you can get paid what you're worth
and live the life that you deserve.

Does it describe? Yes. It says helps people find better-paying jobs.

Does it qualify? Yes, it says she works with high performers who don't feel they're getting paid what they're worth.

Does it disqualify? Yes. If I'm not a high performer, this would not be appealing to me.

Finally, let's look at the example of a Dog Training Coach:

My Perfect Pooch Program
bonds your puppy to you with kindness, not commands
so you can have a loving relationship & an obedient pet.

Does it describe? Yes. We know what she is and what she does. We know how her Perfect Pooch Program is different than traditional dog training.

Does it qualify? Yes, the idea of "kindness, not commands" speaks directly to people who are not comfortable with the idea of dominating their pets.

Does it disqualify? Absolutely. If I believe in the traditional idea of pack hierarchy, where relationships with dogs are formed on status in the pack, this approach will sound like nonsense to me and I'll keep on walking.

Time to write your Bite-Sized Bio. Give yourself some time to create something short, snappy, and that sounds like you.

Using your Bite-Sized Brand Bio

This is a wildly versatile little piece of content. You can copy and paste it in dozens of places, including:

- Your Instagram bio
- Your Facebook bio (in your personal profile too!)
- At the end of your guest blogs
- As an intro when you're on a podcast
- In your email signature
- On the back of your business card
- Verbally—while networking. It can be your "elevator speech"

CHAPTER 3 - **SUMMARY**

- *Your brand is like a house—some components make it stand and function, other components make it attractive to your Best. Client. Ever!*

- *Your **Value Proposition** is the foundation of your Brand House. It clearly outlines your offer and what's unique about you.*

- *Your **Positioning Statement** is the frame and walls of your house. It's what makes your house different from every other house. Your Positioning Statement articulates who you are in relation to your audience, your competitors and in the larger trends affecting your audience.*

- *Your **Brand Voice & Personality** are your window boxes and shutters. It's what gives your brand curb appeal to the right kind of clients. Sharing your Value Proposition and Positioning through the lens of your Brand Voice & Personality will attract the right people and repel the wrong ones.*

- *Your **Brand Origin Story** is the windows and doors on your brand house. It's how people get to look inside, see what you're all about and what makes you tick. The purpose of your Brand Origin Story is to connect with your Best. Client. Ever on a human level by sharing your "why."*

- *Your **Content Mission Statement** is the interior floor plan of the house that tells people what they can expect while interacting with your brand. This is where you tell them what you plan to teach them, both with your free and paid content.*

- *Finally, your **Bite-Sized Brand Bio** acts as a beacon on the roof of your brand house, so those flying overhead can see you from 5,000 feet and identify whether you're right for them or not.*

NOTES

CHAPTER 4:
Minimum Viable Content

By now you're pretty stoked. You've got a handle on your Best. Client. Ever! You've got your brand messaging strategy nailed down. Time to hunker down and get into that big old Content Goldmine, right? Not so fast. Your visibility can't wait until you finish your big project. So let's talk about a Minimum Viable Content Experience so you can get visible now, while you're creating something big and life-changing.

Be seen NOW

OK, so we've nailed down your audience and your brand message. At this point, you're probably thinking it's time to sit down and craft your big, meaty Content Goldmine and not work on anything else until that's done.

And . . . you would be wrong!

One thing that I've seen way too many experts, coaches and consultants do is put their own visibility on hold while they finish up a project.

> *"Well, I don't want to do any social until my website is done... that way I'll have somewhere great to drive people."*

> *"Oh, I'm not going to do any self-promotion until I have a few months of blog content posted. I don't want people to think I haven't been doing this long."*

> *"Right now, I'm working on my course. Until it's done, I have nothing to promote, so there's no point getting out there."*

And my absolute favorite . . .

> *"I'm not doing any social media right now. I'm focusing all my energy on getting clients."*

Word to the wise: You get more clients when people know who the hell you are. Just sayin'.

I'm 100% onboard with the idea of you creating something big and amazing (spoiler alert: that's the whole point of this book). But the idea that you are going to hit pause on all visibility until you've completed and perfected a massive project? That just smacks of fear . . .

Fear of being seen. Fear of being noticed. Fear of being rejected.

And you know what? We are not having that bullshit right now. You are a Real Deal Expert, and you have some Real Deal value to share with people who need you. Do you think those Fake Gurus out there are hitting pause on their social media and podcast guesting? Right. They're full steam ahead.

So, you *will* work on your Content Goldmine. But you will also put together a simple system of visibility so you can start building a following right now, while you're getting the big work done. But the trick is this: it needs to be something you can do in 30–60 minutes per week so you'll stay consistent, and so you'll have time to focus on your big, gorgeous Content Goldmine.

Social media content for an expert, coach or consultant needs to serve four essential functions:

1. Showcase your expertise
2. Establish credibility
3. Build human connections
4. Bring users deeper into a relationship with you

Those functions can all be achieved without a whole lot of fuss.

Enter the Minimum Viable Content Experience.

As someone who's starting a business, you're probably already familiar with the term Minimum Viable Product (MVP). Originally coined in the early 2000s by Frank Robinson, then popularized in Steve Blank and Eric Reis' book *The Lean Startup*, the concept of the MVP has permeated small businesses, allowing them to nail what consumers want in a way that big, bulky, corporate product launches just can't match.

Simply put, a Minimum Viable Product is the most pared-down version possible to still meet the consumer's needs. The MVP is then put into the market, consumers engage with it and provide feedback, and the company iterates on the product and releases an enhanced version. Consumers engage with the enhanced version, provide feedback, and the test-and-learn cycle continues.

The end result? The company doesn't spend a fortune on what it THINKS people want. It spends a little to find out what they truly want, and give them that.

Your Minimum Viable Content Experience will work much the same way. You'll develop a stripped-down strategy to be visible in a limited way on social media with a particular set of topics to test. You'll consistently apply it each week and see what people respond to. From there, you'll be able to incorporate your learning into your Content Goldmine as you create it.

AND . . . you'll be learning while getting some visibility and laying the groundwork for a larger presence later on.

Your Minimum Viable Content Experience will consist of:

- One social media platform
- Five testable content themes
- A pre-built mix of post types
- 30–60 minutes per week
- Weekly assessment

When you consistently apply this technique, essentialist as it is, you'll learn something about your audience every week. You'll discover which topics resonate and which are dogs. You'll create a habit of consistent content creation. And you'll build a following. It will be small and slow-growing at first. But building this while you're creating your Content Goldmine means you'll have someone to launch the Content Goldmine to when it's ready.

And because you've learned so much along the way, that Content Goldmine will be much more in line with what your audience really needs from you. It's a win-win-win-win-win. I think I might have missed a "win," but you get the idea.

The goal of the Minimum Viable Content Experience is to meet the four critical functions of social content in the least amount of time and effort. It doesn't take a major lift to share your expertise, establish credibility, make a connection, and invite people to the next level over the course of the week. Hit those four every week, and move onto other projects.

I highly recommend creating all of the week's social media posts at once, and scheduling them within the platform to post at the desired time, or using a social media management tool like Buffer, Hootsuite, Planoly or whatever you happen to like best.

ONE Platform

This is going to be the first area that I'm going to need you to make a leap away from conventional wisdom with me. Gary Vee and countless others are constantly asserting that you need to be EVERYWHERE on social media. That you need to be on all the newest (unproven) platforms so you can be there first.

As much as I love Gary, this approach is *the* source of most overwhelm and anxiety among experts, coaches and consultants trying to build a personal brand.

We are not building a media empire right now, people. We're about getting you out there in a controlled way, so you can learn while you prep your bigger content platforms.

So I'm not joking about this. Pick ONE social media platform for your Minimum Viable Content experience. Just ONE. Why? Because when you pick more than one, it ceases to be a minimal effort. Our goal here is simplicity and sustainability. We want to streamline this as much as possible and make this as easy for you to continually apply and learn from.

Thus, ONE platform.

Which platform will you pick? That depends on two things:

1. Where your Best. Client. Ever! is hanging out and consuming the type of content that solves their problem.

2. Your level of comfort.

Generally, this is how I look at the main 4 social media platforms:

LinkedIn: You're solving business problems for an ideal client that is a professional at a small or large business. This could be a business owner, but is not a solopreneur, and works in a more traditional vertical (such as finance, human resources, procurement/sourcing). These ideal clients will tend to be over the age of 30.

Instagram: If your ideal client is focused on visual, lifestyle or event-specific needs, and is under the age of 35, and is likely female. If you're a stylist, event planner, caterer, fitness or wellness professional focused on younger clients and you're comfortable producing highly visual content, IG is a good choice.

Facebook: The old standby. If your ideal client is older than 35, a solopreneur or coach, a small business owner, OR you just don't feel like you have a great handle on your ideal client's demographics, this is where you want to start.

Twitter: I will say right now that I hate Twitter. It's a cesspool and it's much harder to get attention there than it used to be. This is the right choice for very few experts, coaches or consultants who have a specific niche to serve. That said, if your ideal client is focused on technology-oriented business or traditional media, you can start here. For everyone else, it's an easy add-on platform later on...but rarely a good starting point.

Now the second criteria for selecting your ONE platform is assessing your level of comfort with that platform. So if your Best. Client. Ever! is an Instagram audience, but you've never really used the platform and are much more comfortable with Facebook, it may feel more comfortable for you to build your Minimum Viable Content Experience on Facebook, than taking your lessons from that platform and translating it to Instagram when you're ready to launch your Content Goldmine.

But if you're feeling ambitious, your audience's needs should trump your own comfort. You can make learning the conventions of Instagram part of your Minimum Viable Content Experience. In this way, you'll be actively learning what works and what doesn't in real-time, as you're building an audience. There's definitely value in that.

One question that comes up frequently is around simultaneous posting. If you're already using a social media management platform like Hootsuite or Buffer or Planoly that allows you to publish to multiple platforms at once, is that OK?

And I would say YES and NO. Yes, it's OK to send ONE post to multiple platforms. No, I don't want you tweaking and optimizing that post for multiple platforms. Doing so defeats the purpose of the ONE platform rule, which is to help you stick to what's essential and avoid what's unnecessary. And right now, what's essential for you is to stick to the platform that's most important to your audience.

At this point, I'm guessing you're pretty clear that I'm serious about the whole ONE platform only thing. The reason we choose only ONE platform is because streamlining that choice allows you to focus on the actual *content strategy* . . . what you intentionally want to put out into the world, and how to bring out ideal clients to us. It is so, so, SO easy to start chasing your tail trying to figure out the best practices on each platform that the first thing to suffer is the actual message. What you want to be known for. What your ideal client most needs from you.

So ONE platform. I'll stop saying that now.

FIVE Testable Themes

What I'm asking you to do here is a tall order for people with deep expertise in their area. I'm asking you to boil down what you know to five general content themes.

Yeah. I know, what you do is much more complicated than that. But for your Minimum Viable Content Experience, it's critical that we keep things simple and streamlined.

For example, I work with a salon coach in Canada. She wants to be known for her deep expertise in her specific vertical, her no-nonsense style, and the massive growth she provides to her clients. What she helps clients with are strategy, mindset, launch events, and referral programs.

Her 5 test themes are:

1. Facts about the salon industry
2. Growth strategy
3. New salon launches
4. Event/product launches at existing salons
5. Driving consistent referrals

All the content around these themes are created in her no-nonsense style and are all infused with plenty of growth stories. But you'll notice that each of her themes serves a specific business purpose—it either showcases her deep expertise or dives into a specific service she offers.
On the other end of the spectrum, I work with a Reiki professional in the Midwest who is putting together a spiritual wellness community for women in their 40s and 50s. Her themes are:

1. Perimenopausal health
2. Money matters

3. Career advancement

4. Love & relationships

5. Spirituality

You can see that her themes are much broader, and focus less on what she offers and more on what matters to her audience, and what topics she wants her community to be known for.

For me, my themes are:

1. Content mindset

2. Brand messaging

3. Content Goldmines (big, meaty content pieces that can fuel a program for a year or more)

4. Content repurposing & process streamlining

5. Long-term content strategy

These are the things I teach, care about, have deep expertise in, and am known for. And most importantly, the people I want to work with need help in these areas.

Why am I keeping you to 5 (and only 5) themes? Because I want you to FOCUS only on creating content that will build your brand in the areas that are aligned with your expertise and that you want to be known for. The different post types will help it not feel repetitive to followers. But remember: you are going to get bored with your content FAR more quickly than your prospects will. You're in it day in and day out and it may feel repetitive to you. Do you know what it feels like to them? It feels consistent. And that's what we want!

As you start to put your Minimum Viable Content Experience into practice, each week you'll focus on a different theme. In a given week, all posts will revolve around that theme. The following week, you'll move to your next theme, and on and on. As a result, you'll be able to learn which themes are most resonant and which get more engagement. And you'll learn which might either need more creative attention, or which just aren't landing. In which case you can lean more heavily into the themes that are working or explore a new theme to replace a dud.

Pick your 5 Themes

Take half an hour to "brain dump" your nerd zone. What are the areas that people really need to understand to learn how to change their lives or businesses with your area of expertise?

If you're a parenting coach, you may find that you can bucket all your topics by age groups:

1. Infants

2. Toddlers

3. Preschoolers

4. School-age kids

5. Teens

Or, you may take a different approach entirely and group your knowledge by the characteristics parents want to instill in their children:

1. Forming connections

2. Discipline

3. Empathy & kindness

4. Responsibility & work ethic

5. Persistence

If you're a financial advisor, you may focus on the five most pressing financial issues you work with clients on:

1. Retirement savings

2. Preserving capital post-retirement

3. College savings

4. Estate planning

5. Charitable giving

Or, you could also focus on the types of people you tend to help:

1. Retirees

2. High-earning professionals

3. Entrepreneurs

4. Young families

5. Women in transition

If you're a life coach, maybe you focus on the mindset issues you address:

1. Fear of not being enough

2. Minimum vs. maximum thinking

3. Victimhood vs. empowerment

4. Boundaries

5. Procrastination

Or, on the other hand, maybe you focus on the transformation tools you use:

1. Vision setting

2. Action planning

3. Journaling

4. Reframing

5. Meditation

You get the idea. There are multiple theme sets that you can break down your area of expertise into, so you'll have a lot of choices. Remember though that you're not committing to these themes for a lifetime. These are topic areas for you to test through your Minimum Viable Content Experience. Don't overthink it. Pick your five test themes and move on.

Your 5 Themes:

....

....

....

....

....

....

....

Congratulations! You've done one of the hardest things in social content creation . . . something most people NEVER do and it's why they continue to struggle.

You've established your swim lanes. You've said I WILL POST ON THIS ONE PLATFORM, AND I WILL POST ABOUT THESE 5 THINGS.

You have already saved yourself a big fat heap of unnecessary work.

The Mix

In the Minimum Viable Content Experience framework, each week represents a test cycle. Each week, you'll pick a different test theme, head over to your one platform of choice and use a prescribed mix of post types to promote your expertise. The post types you'll use:

- **Star Content:** Your primary post for the week, in the form of a livestream, a blog post on your website or a tutorial video

- **Story Posts:** Posts that are all about human connections

- **Starter Posts:** Posts designed to elicit on-platform engagement

- **Step-Up Posts:** Posts designed to get the follower to take action outside of the platform and move deeper into your content ecosystem

We'll dive individually into each of these posts and how to create them, but first I want to show you how you can mix them together to create a week's worth of social content in just 30–60 minutes each Monday.

There are three general options for how you should structure your Minimum Viable Content for each week.

FRONT LOADED	WEEKLY THEME	MONDAY ⭐	TUESDAY	WEDNESDAY
		(Star Content topic)	(Story post topic)	(Starter post topic)
	THURSDAY	FRIDAY	SATURDAY	SUNDAY
	(Step-Up post topic)	(Story post topic)	(Starter post topic)	(Step-Up post topic)

LEAD-UP	WEEKLY THEME	MONDAY	TUESDAY	WEDNESDAY
		(Starter post topic)	(Story post topic)	(Starter post topic)
	THURSDAY	FRIDAY ⭐	SATURDAY	SUNDAY
	(Story post topic)	(Star Content topic)	(Step-Up post topic)	(Step-Up post topic)

	WEEKLY THEME	MONDAY	TUESDAY	WEDNESDAY
SANDWICH		(Story post topic)	(Starter post topic)	(Star Content topic)
	THURSDAY	**FRIDAY**	**SATURDAY**	**SUNDAY**
	(Step-Up post topic)	(Story post topic)	(Starter post topic)	(Step-Up post topic)

You don't have to pick one of these structures and stick with it forever. Some people prefer to post their Star Content on Monday and follow up with the other types of posts. Some people like to do that most of the time, but use a Lead-Up structure when they have something special to launch. Others like the Sandwich Structure so they can have a #Wisdom Wednesday for their Star Content (or just because Wednesday works best for their schedules).

Select the structure that you think will generally work best for your schedule and your preferred working style. But always know that you can revisit as needed.

Star Content

Your Star Content is exactly what it sounds like. It's the center of the week's content universe, the pillar that holds up the whole week's strategy. It's a piece of content that is big enough to anchor the rest of the week's content—setting the theme and serving as either the generator for other posts or the place where all those other posts come together.

In our framework of a Minimum Viable Content Experience built week by week, your Star Content should be small enough for you to create in 20–45 minutes each week, but substantial enough to repurpose for other, smaller content posts (Story posts, Starter posts, and Step-Up posts). The primary purpose of your Star Content is to establish your expertise and build credibility.

Generally, I recommend one of four types of content for your weekly Star Content in a Minimum Viable Content framework:

1. **Livestream:** This is easy to produce and takes just a little planning. Write up your presentation notes and shoot for at least 12 minutes. You can then use your notes to generate ideas for the other posts for the week.

2. **Blog post:** If you already have a blog on your website (even if it's not exactly active), and you're extremely comfortable writing, use the blog for your weekly Star Content. Shoot for a minimum of 500 words on your test topic for the week, then use pieces of what you've written to create the other smaller social posts for the week. On your social platform of choice, you'll link to the blog post AND provide a compelling image and caption that tells people what they'll get out of reading the post.

3. **Downloadable (worksheet, checklist, etc.):** Quick, visual lead magnet that illustrates a concept or provides a useful resource for your audience.

4. **Tutorial video:** If your area of expertise involves more showing than telling, create a weekly tutorial video showing them a tip or trick and why it's useful. You can

house this on your website or YouTube, but ideally, you'd upload the video natively to your one social platform for better visibility (all social platforms prefer native videos to YouTube links).

What you choose should be based on your proficiency and comfort level with certain types of production, and what just naturally brings out your passion for your topic.

If you're more comfortable conveying your ideas out loud rather than through writing, or if you're just super comfy on camera, I highly recommend using a **livestream or video tutorial** as your weekly Star Content. They're fast and easy to produce, and they're highly re-purposable.

If writing is your jam, you can likely crank out 750 words for a **blog post** in 20–45 minutes a week, leaving you plenty of time to create the other post content that comes from that blog post, scheduling those posts, and keeping it under 20 minutes per week.

If you're a natural-born designer, you may prefer building out **downloadable pieces** as your Star Content. But keep in mind that with this option, you'll need a landing page to house it, and that brings a bit of extra work.

When selecting which format you'll use for your Star Content, make sure you're picking a format that:

1. You have generally positive feelings about. If you hate writing, don't pick blog posts. If being on camera makes you want to throw up, opt out of livestreams.

2. You're proficient and efficient in that format—you do it well and you do it quickly.

3. You're confident in the format—you generally feel good about what you produce. Honestly, this last one is optional. You'll get more confident as you create more Star Content. But those first two are mandatory.

In a FRONT-LOADED week, your Star Content happens at the beginning of the week. You can use quotes from your Star piece to create social graphics for the other posts later in the week, or just take concepts from your Star Content and ask questions about them for your Starter posts.

In a LEAD-UP week, your Star Content comes at the end, and can include many of the points you used in earlier posts, and anything you learned from those posts. For example, if you're an expert in interior design, if one of your Starter posts earlier in the week asked people what neutral they've been gravitating toward these days, you can use the resulting conversations as part of your Star Content—either as an infographic, or just quoting some of the things people have said.

Your Star Content is where you'll be showcasing your expertise for the week. You know your format, you know your theme, and for the most part, that should be enough to get you started creating. If not, head back over to the very nifty **AnswerThePublic.com** and enter your theme word. It will give you a bunch of questions and common search terms that are excellent content ideas around your theme.

Your Star Content acts as the mother post for the week. It can be broken up and repurposed to make the other pieces.

Story Posts

I'm sure you've heard plenty of Fake Gurus (and some real ones) talk about how "storytelling" is essential when it comes to marketing your business and establishing your expertise and status as a thought leader. But nobody ever really tells you how to do it specifically for a social post.

The Story Post has one primary purpose—to connect you to your followers. The first priority of a Story Post is to get your followers to know, like, and trust you. If the story is about one of your client's success, then there's a secondary purpose: building credibility.

Each week, your Story Post will be directly and closely connected to your Star Content. The Story Post will illustrate that topic in a way people can easily understand.

Let's take for example an executive coach I know. Her theme of the week is Negotiation. Her Star Content was a blog post on 4 negotiation tactics for women that won't impact their "likeability."

In this case, she has a couple of potential stories. One could be a story about a client who implemented one of the tactics, got a higher salary, and was viewed by leadership as a superstar thereafter.

The coach could also write a story about HERSELF. Maybe the reason she got into executive coaching is because she was sick of seeing crazy-smart women being undervalued by their companies, and that learning negotiating skills completely empowered her to change the game for herself—and she wanted to do the same for other women.

That's a short version of a "Brand Origin Story." It doesn't build credibility in the exact same way as a client success story because it isn't sharing proof that what you do works. But it DOES build credibility by sharing your intentions, your passion, and your personal experience. A Story Post about you helps followers to know, like, and trust you.

Story structure in a social post

While I don't think we need to walk through the entire 9-stage Hero's Journey structure in a social post, I find a pared-down version of this extremely effective. Think of your Story Post in these 5 stages:

- The sucky point A

- Why it hurt so much to be there

- The turning point

- The actions taken

- The amazing point B

For example, take a look at this Story Post that a fitness coach wrote about one of her clients (it was accompanied by an awesome photo of the client).

Ladies, can I just take a moment today to recognize Amber?

When I met Amber, she was so far down in a hole, you couldn't even see her natural sparkle. She was more than 100 pounds above her normal weight.

She didn't have energy to play with her kids. She wouldn't apply for promotions at work because she didn't want to call attention to herself. Her back and knees hurt whenever she had to walk anywhere. Y'all, she refused to wear shorts. In Alabama. In July.

It was rough.

One night after a tough day at work, Amber asked her son if he wanted to play Xbox with her. He said he really wanted to ride bikes . . . "But you can't do that, can you Mom?"

Her heart stopped. No. She couldn't.

The very next day Amber called me. We talked about all of it. She was truly a woman possessed—ready to take control of her body and get to a place where it wasn't stopping her from living the life she deserved . . . that her kids deserved.

So I started her on the 14-week program. And she just went into full-on beast mode.

TRUE STORY: You give this woman a plan, and she just goes for it! It's been an absolute joy to be part of her journey!

Fast-forward to today. Amber is 8 weeks into her journey. And she's ditched 26 of those pounds. 26, y'all!

She's riding a bike with her kids (who are totally thrilled!). She's speaking up at work. She's laughing so much more! Her back and knees don't hurt anymore. She feels younger, more energetic, and is getting so much more out of life.

Amber, THANK YOU so much for calling me that day, and giving me the honor of joining you on your journey. It's been a blessing in my life!

Do you see how in that social story the coach starts with Amber's pain? Then she moves through her turning point, the actions she took, and her amazing end state. The coach sandwiched this story structure between two important points—**recognition and thanks**. This shows her prospects how they can expect to be treated as clients.

Because Amber was tagged in the post (which she consented to), her friends were able to see how she was getting such great results, creating more visibility for the coach.

If you DON'T have client consent to tell their stories, you can still tell the stories without a name.

Beyond the 5-step structure, remember to keep your paragraphs short. Like one sentence short. Long paragraphs don't play well in any of the social media platforms.

The trouble with stories . . .

Time for a little real talk. Nearly every client I have worked with has struggled with Story Posts. There's something about the word "story" that freaks people out. Especially really smart people who don't necessarily consider themselves creative.

I remember one client telling me she couldn't use her story on social media. "I already have that story on my website," she said. "People already know it."

But that's the thing: you have more than one story. You have millions of stories that play into who you are, why you're great at what you do, and why it matters to you. And the great news is that you've already written your master story—your Brand Origin Story.

Let's think back to the example Brand Origin Story we worked with in the last chapter. If you were to disassemble that story by each stage of the Hero's Journey, you'd find several shorter, more focused stories that illustrate critical points. Here are five different examples of ways you could riff on that story . . . and how you can repurpose and remix your own story.

Remix 1: Reliving the Call to Adventure

Projecting yourself back to when you were still in "the normal world," before the call to adventure came, before you remade your life is highly relatable to those who are currently deciding whether to follow their own call.

There was a time when I would hit the snooze button eight times before wearily dragging myself into the shower.

A time when I had to psych myself up to get in the car and drive to work. I'd come home exhausted, numb out with some TV and chips, go to bed too late, and wake up to do it all over again the next day.

My job wasn't terrible. There was no toxic boss. No massive overwork. But I had long mastered my responsibilities, and the prospect of 'moving up' more than I had held zero appeal for me.

I just didn't care about the work. And I couldn't see how doing this same joyless thing day after day would help me find my purpose.

Maybe I needed to be in the state I was in. That dull, lifeless aching for more—more meaning, more challenge, more power to impact the world.

Maybe it's because I was in such a low place that I took that first call. A friend who wanted me to step out of my comfort zone and do some volunteer strategic planning with a local nonprofit.

Not a year before, I would have declined because I was too busy striving and climbing.

But in that moment, as dissatisfied as I was with my place in the world, as completely clueless as I was about how to build a life that lit me up, I saw this as an opportunity.

And if I hadn't taken it, my life never would have changed.

Friends, if you're in that place where you're searching for purpose and you don't yet know how to find it . . . this time has meaning for you. It opens you up to opportunities to grow. Opportunities that you can't see when you're in full-on beast mode.

As hard as it is, be grateful for this time. Long after your call comes, you'll recognize that it was now, these long, empty days when your transformation began.

Now you try this type of remix for your own Brand Origin Story:

Remix 2: Trial & Failure/Growth & New Skills

Sharing the story of the trials and failures does a few things. First, it gives your clients a realistic picture of the path ahead of them. Second, it underscores your authority by showing that you've paid your dues. And finally, it just makes you easier to like. People can relate more easily to someone who has failed, can admit their failure, and who keeps getting back up to fight.

> *There was nothing like the feeling of leaving a strategy session with my clients when I first got started.*
>
> *It was such a high. I was HELPING. I was impacting the way high-value organizations did critical work in the world.*
>
> *But as high as that high was, after a few months, I was smacked in the face with a low I hadn't planned for.*
>
> *My clients weren't implementing. They weren't changing. And I was failing.*
>
> *Over and over again, those strategy sessions I put my heart and soul into and felt so good about was doing a whole lot of NOTHING. All I was doing was taking people away from their work for a day, so they could go back the next day and make zero changes.*
>
> *Devastation. I felt like such a fraud. And the word was starting to spread. There was really no point for any nonprofit in my market to work with me.*
>
> *Holy smokes, how do you even come back from that?*
>
> *For me, it took a lot of soul-searching. And a lot of (sometimes unwilling) mindset work. but I had a great coach who dragged me kicking and screaming.*
>
> *And I wrestled with a whole marching band of gnarly thoughts . . . That I was an idiot. That my clients were just*

lazy. That I never should have gone into this business. Who the hell did I think I was anyway???

It was a low-down low, let me just tell you.

The mindset work is what ultimately brought me to a model of accountability that ended up working for my clients. But getting there was . . . rough.

The failure is where your work begins. It's what opens your eyes to new possibilities. It's where you find your strength and your way forward.

It was for me. I know it's almost cliche to talk about how good failure is.

WHEN YOU'RE IN IT, IT SO DOES NOT FEEL GOOD.

But if you're willing to fight through, there's a world of possibilities waiting for you. You just can't see them unless failure's forcing you to.

So that's my wish for all of you today. Failure will come. May you find the vision to make it as productive and transformative as possible.

Now you give it a try:

_____

_____

_____

_____

_____

_____

Remix 3: Your Mentor

Talking about the Mentor who led you into the unknown is a way to help others looking for a Guide to see themselves in your transformation . . . and even start thinking about you as the Guide. Who changed your life? How did they do it? And how did you find them?

> When I fell into my first nonprofit consulting gig, I didn't expect to fall in love. But I did.
>
> And my first thought was, "OMG, I do not have the nonprofit bona fides for anyone to trust me. It's time to get some help."
>
> So a quick internet search led me to Sadie. She had been doing the same kind of consulting with the same kind of clients for 22 years.
>
> And her reputation was stellar. I will admit that even setting up time with her was super intimidating. She was the QUEEN of the field that I was just starting in.
>
> Why would she want to spend her valuable time giving up her hard-earned knowledge for a wannabe like me?
>
> But she was overjoyed to talk. She LOVES talking about this stuff.
>
> And that's the thing I learned about people who are in this for the right reasons. They are so just head over heels with their area of expertise, they'll share that expertise with anyone. And love every second of it.
>
> And you know what? It paid off for her. I became a coaching client of hers for six years. It was the expertise, sure. But what really sold me was the love.

So when you're wondering if you're giving too much away, or whether you really have time to talk to someone who's interested in learning from you, just remember this:

The love you have for your work is what makes people pick you as a Guide. Because they have that love too. And that's why they're talking to you.

Give this angle a go:

_____

_____

_____

_____

_____

_____

_____

_____

_____

_____

_____

_____

_____

_____

_____

_____

_____

Remix 4: Revelation

Dive deeper into the story of your aha moment. The realization that changed everything for you is what many of your audience is still on their way to. They're still meeting the Guide and are in trial and failure. They need to know that the revelation is still out there. That the trial and failure areall worth it. And that they'll come out on the other side stronger.

> *The lowest point in my business was when it became clear that my model was having no impact.*
>
> *No matter how hard I tried, no matter how much research I did, how much tweaking, how much pushing, how much pulling . . .*
>
> *It. Didn't. Work.*
>
> *I was ineffective. In my life, I have never worked so hard, just to have zero impact.*
>
> *Once I realized it was the organizational MINDSET that was keeping clients from implementing the model, the struggle stopped.*
>
> *I could see how everything fit. The path was clear, and what I needed to do to move down that path made me feel lighter than air.*
>
> *There was no more pushing, pulling, grinding, tearing my hair out.*
>
> *It was clarity. And a giddy excitement to keep moving down that road, to a place where my impact was certain.*
>
> *BUT: I could not have gotten there without the pushing, pulling, grinding, tearing my hair out.*
>
> *I couldn't have hit the AHA! without the heartache. And neither can you.*

So if you're deep in the grind right now and can't see a way out, keep going. It's there.

The grind is part of your journey the same way it was part of mine.

It sucks, to be sure. But trust the process and proceed with faith that you're moving in the right direction.

Your turn!

Remix 5: What it's like to return home changed

Explore the end of the story. What is it like to bring back everything you've learned home? Is it hard to relate in the same way to people still in the normal world? How are you able to impact the normal world with what you've learned? How do you see things differently and are able to better enjoy the normal world? There are dozens of ways to tell this story.

Do you know what the best part of this job is? Now that I've finally gotten it right?

Things that used to be major inconveniences are now some of my biggest sources of joy.

When I got to cook dinner and OOPS! We're missing a major ingredient. Let's just go out to our favorite Mexican joint! We have the time and the money, so let's just do it.

When the basement flooded because the sump pump malfunctioned? Score! Let's just redo the basement! We wanted to anyway and now we have an excuse . . . AND a little insurance money to help!

When my daughter gets a cold, instead of bemoaning the fact that I won't get to work that day, I enjoy snuggling up in our PJs and watching Harry Potter movies all day.

Having control over my time, the income to keep us comfortable, and the mindset that little things are just NBD has changed everything.

It can change for you too. If your nonprofit is struggling with nonstop work and STILL not enough money coming in to have the impact you want, I can help.

It won't just change your organization— it can change your life!

Try this one now:

The thing to remember is that these are just examples. They're written in the very specific voice of the consultant. Yours will be in a different voice—your voice.

Hopefully, that helps clear up Story Posts, gives you plenty of ideas to get started, and provides the confidence you need to just put yourself out there. Your story is worth telling. Your story is how you became an expert. Feed it to people a bit at a time and let them see the emotion behind it. That's how we make connections. That's how you build trust before you ever meet someone.

Starter Posts

The purpose of a Starter Post is to start a conversation with your audience. The goal here is two-fold: when you generate engagement with the post, your later content is more likely to be seen by users on the platform. And, by starting conversations with people, you're deepening that connection (remember those critical functions of social content? That's one of 'em!).

Now, I've seen plenty of Starter Posts that focus on what I call mindless engagement. It's engagement that has nothing to do with your area of expertise.

You know, those "show me a pic of your dog" or "which quarantine house would you live in?" posts?

I'm not a fan . . .

If our goal is stripping away the non-essential elements of social content so you can start building a presence and learn what about your expertise most excites your audience, then mindless engagement is not on the table for you.

But there are conversation starters that have EVERYTHING to do with your business, your offering, and the problems you solve for clients.

Here's an example from a writing coach who helps new novelists get their first works published:

The coach kicked things off by talking about the author she envied as the post text, and talked about why she so loved that author's style. The post generated responses from followers who weren't yet clients, and gave the coach a way to see who really was longing to write something. It gave her some fantastic ammunition for follow-up communications.

Here's another example from a life coach who focuses on moving people out of their comfort zones:

What's ONE new thing you can try this weekend? Even the tiniest thing?

This one didn't even require going into Canva. It took about 20 seconds to post and generated 30+ conversations with followers. And the coach got to see where they were in their journeys, which gave her excellent ideas for how to approach them.

Polls, "this or that" posts that ask users to choose one option over another, and "caption this" posts are other ways to engage people with Starter-style Posts.

Starter Posts are all about engagement. Getting people to comment on your post so they'll continue to see your stuff in their feed, and so your posts will be shown to more people. That's the more-eyeballs benefit to engagement.

The more powerful benefit, in my opinion, is that you get to learn more about the people who are watching you and spot some potential Best. Clients. Ever!

Your Starter Posts should take you about a minute or two to create. They're fast. They're easy. And even though they don't pack the content-heavy punch of a Story Post, they're little powerhouses. The engagement driven by your Starter Posts helps make sure the rest of your content gets seen. Don't overlook these.

Step-Up Posts

This is where the action is. A Step-Up Post is when you ask your follower to . . . well, to step up. You want them to take action to deepen your relationship.

This can be setting up a consult call, buying a low-ticket offer, joining a group, registering for an event, showing up at your livestream . . . really, it's whatever next action is most important to your business.

The Step-Up Post must urge them to take that action with clear next steps. There are three general actions you can ask people to take in Step-Up Posts:

1. Link them to an action step (opt-in form, registration page, or scheduling page). For example: *WOOHOO! My new book is finally available for pre-order! Get your name down before these bad boys sell out! (Accompanied by a photo of the book and a link to pre-order.)*

2. Ask for a comment as permission to send them something (this type of Step-Up gets post engagement AND a next action that allows you into their DMs). For example: *We've just completed a new retirement planning checklist. Give me a $ if you want a copy.*

3. Participate in an on-platform event (view a livestream, participate in a Q&A). Example: *I'm going live in 30 minutes to answer all your questions on the Autoimmune Protocol. Join me here at 1pm PT.*

These are your promo posts. And in the Minimum Viable Content Experience framework, we follow the 2:1. You should only have 1 purely promotional post for every 2 value-adding posts you create.

Weekly Assessment

Each week, take a look at how your posts performed. What you're looking for is engagement in terms of comments and link clicks. Likes don't matter. Ask yourself:

- How did my Star Content perform compared to past weeks?

- How did all the week's posts compare to past weeks?

- Did my engagement posts yield any fruitful learning?

- Did my Step-Up Posts generate the desired actions (opt-ins, registrations, appointments, permission to DM a resource, etc.)?

- How did my Step-Up Posts compare to past weeks?

Week after week, you'll see that certain topics and certain formats perform better than others. After a quarter, sit down and retool your 5 Themes based on what you learned. Maybe lean heavily into some post types that are performing better for you by adding more of them into your weekly schedule. This is a simple way to learn and respond, and it doesn't require a ton of overthinking.

Quality of writing

This should go without saying, but I'm going to say it anyway. Please proofread your social posts. I don't believe everything has to be perfect. Imperfection can be endearing. But obvious typos and misspellings do impact your credibility. So double check. And if you notice that something wrong after it's posted, you can correct it. Y'all, I've posted more typos and mistakes than I care to mention. It's going to happen and it is not the end of the world. But a little double checking goes a long way to make sure mistakes are the exception, rather than the rule.

CHAPTER 4 - **SUMMARY**

- *Don't wait until your Content Goldmine is done to start producing high-value social media content. Get out there now with the Minimum Viable Content Experience Framework.*

- *Select only ONE social media platform to focus on and FIVE topic areas within your expertise that you want to be known for.*

- *Each week, you'll build a mix of social content from one piece of Star Content, 2 Story Posts, 2 Starter Posts, and 2 Step-Up Posts.*

- *This mix of posts will enable you to easily, effortlessly achieve the four core objectives of social content:*

  o *Sharing your expertise*

  o *Building credibility*

  o *Creating connections*

  o *Driving action*

- *Build out all the week's social content at once, scheduling it to run at the desired time in a social media management tool or directly in the platform.*

- *Each week, look at the performance of your posts compared to previous weeks to see which topics and formats generate the most action.*

NOTES

Creating Your
Content Goldmine

This is the part that's been freaking you out since you learned about the Content Goldmine model.

Yes, I really expect you to create a hefty piece of content—most likely an eBook that's rich enough to mine content from for a year.

Yes, you can do this in a matter of weeks.

And yes, if it sounds like too much, it's unbelievably easy to outsource.

So no more freaking out. Let's get the damn thing done!

What's a Content Goldmine?

The Content Goldmine is a one long-form, meaty piece of content that you put effort into upfront. It gets written, designed, approved—and then you mine the content within it and repurpose it in multiple different ways. It's a content piece with a thud factor, like an eBook or original research report or an online course.

Your Content Goldmine lives within a landing page—a web page that is specifically set up to give people access to the Content Goldmine in exchange for an email address. That email address is your primary objective. As you'll recall from Chapter 1, the Content Goldmine is at the heart of the content marketing model we'll be using because it is rich enough for you to easily mine fuel 9–12 months' worth of shorter-form content—your Gold Bars content.

Now, as you're preparing to create your Content Goldmine, there are four critical questions you need to answer:

1. What exact topic/angle my Content Goldmine deal with?

2. What format should my Content Goldmine be?

3. What should I name my Content Goldmine?

4. Who's going to create my Content Goldmine? Me or someone else?

Once you answer these questions, you're ready to get into it. And remember, the whole time you're creating your Content Goldmine, your Minimum Viable Content Experience should be cranking right along, providing you good insights about your Best. Client. Ever! and starting to build your following.

Finding Your Content Sweet Spot

Believe it or not, you've already done most of the hard work when it comes to finding your content sweet spot and selecting the right topic for your Content Goldmine. The work you've put in on understanding your Best. Client. Ever! and figuring out those keywords that are most appealing to them will come front and center right now, as will your competitive research and brand Value Proposition.

Take a moment to re-familiarize yourself with those pieces of your strategy.

Now, when we talk about the content sweet spot, we're talking about where your Value Proposition overlaps with what your Best. Client. Ever! needs most. That's the sweet spot you're looking for. If you can find a topic that ALSO overlaps with competitive white space, you're in Unicorn territory (for the record, I've never seen this happen, so if you find a genuine Unicorn topic, let me know and I'll buy you a steak or impossible burger or something).

Now, you may notice that you find a couple of areas that align with your Differentiators and Game Changers that competitors aren't talking about. This is exciting . . . until you realize you can find no evidence that your Best. Client. Ever! gives a hoot about it. When this happens, you're solidly in "irrelevant" territory.

You may also come across situations where you find something that your Best. Client. Ever! cares about quite a bit that none of your competitors are addressing. The only problem? You're not addressing it either. That's actually not a problem at all . . . it's a massive opportunity. There's a potential land-grab in unicorn territory if you're willing to tweak your offering.

Take some time to go through the topic areas you've settled on in your Minimum Viable Content Experience and the keywords you identified as important to your Best. Client. Ever! Use the table below to score each of your ideas based on each of the items across the top, on a scale of 1–10. When you're done, add up all the numbers for each content idea to give each idea a final score. The content idea with the highest score should be your starting point.

Topic idea	Solves a problem	Matters to prospect	Aligns to your brand	Competitive white space	Total score

Looks like you just found your sweet spot . . . and the topic for your first Content Goldmine.

Choosing a Content Goldmine Format

When it comes to creating your first Content Goldmine, you have 4 basic choices:

- eBook
- Original Research Report
- An Actual Book
- An Online Course

Types of Content Goldmines

EBOOK

Best place to start

- 50+ pages
- Establishes authority on a topic
- Comprehensive overview
- Requires some research
- Organized "braindump" of expertise

REAL-DEAL BOOK

Big effort, big reward

- More work to secure publishing or self-publish
- Super mineable
- Doesn't always lend itself to the Content Goldmine model unless it's set up to
- Can't easily be given for an email address
- Is a sellable product

ORIGINAL RESEARCH

- Content marketing unicorn
- Drives a lot of leads
- Generates media inquiries
- Requires original research
- A lot of data = a lot of design required
- Generates infographics

COURSE

- Ideal if you already have several presentations or a seminar you teach
- Only workable if it's in-depth enough to mine
- Can use content bites to sell course

While each has its pros and cons, my recommendation is typically to start with an eBook if it's your first time out. It doesn't have the additional steps of securing a publisher or dealing with the whole self-publishing rigamarole, so it's much easier than a real book. And there's no primary research required—likely, any secondary research you'll be using for an eBook is something you're already familiar with (because after all, you know your subject area pretty damn well).

The Original Research Report is also an excellent place to start. There is more work on the front end because, in addition to secondary research that's already been published, you'll need to conduct your own primary research, usually in the form of a survey. What's great about an Original Research Report though, is that you'll end it with new statistics, maybe some that are unexpected that you can pitch to the media.

For example, if you're a financial advisor in Pittsburgh, and you only serve local clients, you could publish an original research report on the state of wealth and retirement savings in Pittsburgh. The local focus and specific and timely revelations will be very attractive to local traditional media, which will go a long way in helping get you known in the local market and develop relationships with reporters.

On the back end, once you have all your data for your research report, you'll want to invest the time and money in having the data points designed in a clean, modern, easy to read way. Consumers have high expectations of data visualization, so this isn't something you can half-ass. If you commit to doing an Original Research Report, commit to outsourcing the design work so you can make it a quality product.

If you already have a book published, this can serve as your Content Goldmine. If you don't, I wouldn't recommend this for your first time out. The same goes for podcasts—if you already have a weekly podcast with some traction, that can serve as your Content Goldmine. We'll talk about how to break down podcast episodes into other types of content in the next chapter.

And finally, there's the Online Course. If you already have multiple presentations that you share or an ongoing seminar that you teach, this could be an option for you. It's more challenging than an eBook or Original Research Report because it requires more technology alignment—a course delivery platform, video hosting, video editing, quality mics and lights. So this wouldn't be my pick for first-timers either. Our goal here is to pick something that you can finish quickly, start mining, and get out into the world and in front of your Best. Client. Ever!

Naming Your Content Goldmine

For the meat of your Content Goldmine title, I want you to take another look at the search terms associated with the topic you chose. Now that you've settled on a topic, you may want to run it through AnswerThePublic.com or SEMRush again to find related search terms that have high volume. Decide how you want to word your topic based on the search terms.

Now, when it comes to turning a search term into a title for your Content Goldmine, you want something that sounds comprehensive, useful, and like it will solve a problem. Here are some thoughts for building out your title:

- The Ultimate Guide to (search term/topic)
- The (search term/topic) Roadmap
- The (search term/topic) Blueprint
- How to (solve a problem) in 30 Days
- The (search term/topic/problem) Guidebook
- The (search term/topic/problem) Field Guide
- State of the (search term/topic) Industry (This would be an Original Research Report)
- The (search term/topic) Handbook
- The (search term/topic) Playbook
- The (search term/topic) Game Plan
- The Step-by-Step (search term/topic) Plan

Do some brainstorming around your Content Goldmine name. Take your favorites and do a quick Google search to see if anyone else in your field is using that name or something similar. If you have more than one that you like, ask your Best. Clients. Ever! in some of the Facebook groups or subReddits you've identified and get their take. Sometimes they'll validate your favorite, sometimes they'll pick one that you really don't like, and crystallize which direction you really wanted to begin with. Either way, you learn something.

To do or not to do?

The gorgeous thing about a Content Goldmine is that even though it's big, it's still just one piece. But it's one piece that needs to be written, proofed and designed. Many experts will want to do this themselves (and I'm all for that). This gives you the practice you need to hone your voice and really distill some of your ideas into formal frameworks.

But it is just as valid an option to outsource this piece. Finding a reputable freelancer or content agency to take on this project for you will take a load off your shoulders. You can keep rolling with your Minimum Viable Content Experience, wooing clients, taking care of your current clients, with the knowledge that someone else is doing the heavy lifting on this. You'll likely have to fact check, proofread, make style and voice suggestions, but it is much easier.

In order to successfully outsource a piece of this magnitude (both in size and in impact to your overall content program), you'll want to take some careful steps upfront to make sure you're happy with the finished project.

- **Focus on quality writing.** Don't just go on Fiverr and find the cheapest possible person to write your content. Ask other experts. Get references. Find someone familiar with your nerd zone so you're not having to completely educate them about what you do. Ask for writing samples.

- **Brief your resource thoroughly.** Provide your freelancer or agency with your Brand Messaging Strategy and samples of your social content so they understand your voice, Value Proposition, Positioning, etc. Ideally, you will have at least outlined the Content Goldmine so your resource is crystal clear on what content you want to be included.

- **Know what you're paying for.** If you go with a freelancer, you'll likely have to hire a writer and a designer separately. If you go with an agency, it's one scope of work for the whole job. You may think that an agency will automatically be more expensive, but the struggle of managing two freelancers may be worth bypassing if you're very busy. Consider agencies in less expensive areas, like the Midwest, that you can work with remotely.

Whichever you decide—outsourcing or doing it yourself— remember that the goal here is to get the damn thing done. Letting it linger on the periphery of consciousness in a half-done state just sucks mental energy away from everything else you're doing. Bang it out. And if it's easier to bang it out with help from professional writers and designers, then do that. The only states of progress with a Content Goldmine are DONE and NOT DONE. We want you to get DONE.

eBooks

If you're choosing to write an eBook, good choice! It's a great starter Content Goldmine for your first time out, and it offers you plenty of room to showcase the depth of your expertise.

The purpose of your eBook, whether it's an ultimate guide style or a more "how-to" focused piece, is to solve a problem for your Best. Client. Ever! It's with the purpose of problem-solving in mind that you're going to structure your eBook. The job of the eBook is to take your reader from point A to point B. Point A is where they are now—currently mired in the problem they need you to help solve. Point B is where the problem is solved.

Let's be clear: is the eBook going to completely solve the problem? No. But what it will do is show them the path to solving it, the knowledge required, and most importantly, that you know exactly how to get them there.

Back to point A and point B. Between these two points, there are several things that your reader needs to know. I would like you to identify what those milestones are. What are the critical things that the reader needs to know or accomplish in order to move from point A to point B? Shoot for around 8 milestones (no more than 10, no fewer than 6).

The Milestones

Each of these milestones is a chapter in your eBook. So the eBook outlined above would have 8 chapters.

Within each chapter, there are going to be pieces of information that your reader needs or tasks that they need to accomplish in order to achieve the milestone associated with that chapter. These are the sections of your chapter. Ideally, you'll want 5–7 sections within each chapter, each section covering something that your reader needs to know, understand or achieve in order to complete that milestone.

1	2	3	4	5	6	7	8
• Item 1	• Item 1	• Item 1	• Item 1	• Item 1	• Item 1	• Item 1	• Item 1
• Item 2	• Item 2	• Item 2	• Item 2	• Item 2	• Item 2	• Item 2	• Item 2
• Item 3	• Item 3	• Item 3	• Item 3	• Item 3	• Item 3	• Item 3	• Item 3
• Item 4	• Item 4	• Item 4	• Item 4	• Item 4	• Item 4	• Item 4	• Item 4
• Item 5	• Item 5	• Item 5	• Item 5	• Item 5	• Item 5	• Item 5	• Item 5
• Item 6		• Item 6	• Item 6			• Item 6	• Item 6

Before you write one word of your eBook, you will want to map out your Chapters and Sections. You can do it with sticky notes on your wall, you can draw it out on a whiteboard . . . you can carve it into a stone tablet if that's how you roll. But one way or another, mapping out the framework of the eBook first will give you your best chance to complete it.

Even if you're planning to outsource the project—because this is your expertise we're talking about here—I strongly recommend mapping out your Chapters and Sections to give to your content creator.

Now, once you've mapped out your Chapters and Sections, something magical happens to the process of creating this thing. You're no longer looking at sitting down to create a MASSIVE, HUGE, eBOOK. You're going to sit down and create a Section. It's a much more manageable way to look at the work, and a far less intimidating way to plan the work than just writing on your to-do list "write Rheumatoid Arthritis eBook." I promise you that to-do item will never get crossed out if you don't map out your Chapters and Sections. Doesn't it sound much more doable to see "Write Section on Autoimmune Protocol?" Anybody can sit down and write a Section.

An eBook is absolutely a big project. But it's like eating an elephant. How do you eat an elephant? One bite at a time. And your Sections are your bites.

Ideally, each Section should be about 750 words. Generally, you want no less than 500 and no more than 1,250. Keep in mind that each Section should be able to act as a stand-alone blog post once you get into Gold Bar content territory.

Important note: Take a look at the keyword research you initially did to get to know your Best. Client. Ever! Are there search terms you found there that naturally fit within your Chapters and Sections? Once you've mapped out your Chapters and Sections, make your way over to Answer ThePublic.com and SEMRush to find at least one search term that best fits each Chapter and Section. This will be important for titling the Sections, and when we're breaking down each piece into Gold Bar Content.

What else do you need in your eBook?

With your Chapters and Sections mapped out, let's talk about the connective tissue of an eBook that makes it feel like a cohesive piece. Other items you'll want to create to pull everything together include:

- **Cover:** This will include your title and subtitle, plus your name, logo and website.

- **Introduction:** Your intro should run about 500 words, and tell people why you felt it was important to write the eBook, and what problem it will solve. The introduction is a great place to pull in a client story or anecdote.

- **Table of Contents:** Show each Chapter and provide a page number.

- **Chapter Dividers:** At the beginning of each chapter, have a divider page with the Chapter title and 100–250 words about what they can expect to come away with in each chapter.

- **Conclusion:** 500-word recap of what the reader learned, why it was important, and what they should do with the information. You can also pull a client story or anecdote in here.

- **About the Author:** Copy and paste that lovely Brand Origin Story here.

- **Next Steps:** This is the call-to-action for the Content Goldmine. It's a whole page dedicated to telling the reader how they can work with you.

Next Steps page

The purpose of this page is to guide the reader into how they can work with you more closely. Whether that's through an online course, a group challenge or coaching program, or 1:1 coaching (or all 3!), this is the page you'll want to list out all of those possibilities and include clickable links (and easy-to-type URLs for those who print this out) so they can access those services.

For the title, you can just use Next Steps, or something that speaks more to your personality.

Examples: *Next steps*
                Ready to keep going?
                Your growth doesn't end here

Think of each call to action as a chunk. It's OK to have 4–5 chunks on a page. It's OK to have 1 chunk on a page. As you add products or ways to work with you, you can come back and add them to this page.

Example chunk: *1:1 Coaching*
                   Are you ready to work with me on a deeper level, with regular 1:1 sessions that are customized to your unique needs? <u>Reach out</u> now and select Life Mapping Session so we can discuss your transformation.
                   (Insert an easy web address)

                   5-Day Bootcamp Challenge
                   Want to take this learning a step further? New Bootcamp Challenges are starting soon. Learn more and <u>join the next group.</u> now to put what you've learned into practice.
                   (Insert an easy web address)

In the end, your Next Step page will be laid out like this:

Title:

CTA chunks: *(label)*
               (short description and linked text)
               (easy URL)

Your website:

Your FB group:

Your other social profiles:

Your phone number and email address:

Original Research Reports

If you've committed to creating an Original Research Report as your Content Goldmine, you've made a bit of extra work for yourself. But don't worry—the time spent gathering insights will not only yield an in-demand piece, but it will also teach you boatloads about your Best. Client. Ever!

Your first step in creating an Original Research Report is (wait for it) . . . the research. But you knew that already. So, does that mean you're going to put together a list of survey questions of everything you want to know about your topic area and put it out into the world?

Nope!

We're going to work a bit counter intuitively here. Before you send out a single survey, you're going to ask yourself what data points you want to include in the report. Why this approach? Because you're coming to this with a point of view. You know there are stats that would be particularly interesting, compelling and eye-opening. You want to make sure you build your questions so your survey respondents are giving you the data you need to make those stats happen.

One drawback: you may have a hypothesis that a high percentage of your audience feels or behaves in a certain way about something. They may prove you wrong. That info is just as valuable (and probably just as eye-opening and with as much media appeal if it goes against conventional wisdom).

Ask yourself if there are interesting, thought-provoking ideas in your vertical that don't yet have stats to prove or disprove them.

Are there stats that are particularly relevant to your Differentiator or Game Changer offerings? For example, if you are an accountant who offers a Start-Up package to new businesses to help them get their accounting systems in order, it's probably worth finding out if accounting inaccuracies or bad bookkeeping is putting a lot of strain on start-ups during their critical first years.

And of course, don't overlook stats that would be highly informative or entertaining to your audience, even if it's not perfectly aligned with one of your core themes. Does your audience find it interesting that people in their particular field drink more coffee than any other? That most people in their type of business who fail do so because they didn't advertise enough? That most moms like the ones you serve are more stressed out managing their husbands than their kids? Think about what answers would be the most interesting, and ask your respondents about that.

Your Survey

This is a piece that can be outsourced, but survey research is still an expensive thing to hire out. I strongly recommend doing this yourself using SurveyMonkey.

First, develop your questions. For each data point you want to illuminate, create 1 or 2 questions that will give you clear answers. Include a few open-ended questions as well where respondents share how they feel about something or their experiences. You can pull quotes from these responses and use them as graphics that add color and texture to your finished report.

At the end of the survey, ask respondents to share their email address if they'd like to see the results. It's a great way to build your list, and if they took the survey, chances are they'll want to see how it turns out.

When it comes to respondents, you'll want at least 250. That may sound like a lot, but in order to get the quantity of data to make the survey legitimate, this is your baseline. There are multiple free ways to find survey respondents (Facebook Groups and subReddits that serve your prospects, your existing clients and email list, industry associations who might be willing to partner with you). But cobbling together respondents in this way might be more time-consuming an endeavor than you're looking for.

SurveyMonkey offers a service called SurveyMonkey Audience. The service allows you to choose how many respondents you want, and select criteria for the respondents (age, income, education, occupation, etc.). SurveyMonkey then puts together a survey cohort for you and delivers your survey to them. You pay per completion. Generally, you can expect this to cost a few hundred dollars, but it will give you the results you want in a matter of 7–10 days.

Creating Your Report

When your survey results come back, take your time going through the results. Read all the open-ended responses and make note of any particularly powerful findings. From there, you'll want to organize your findings into 6–8 themes. Each of these themes will be a Section of your report.

Within each Section, each data point will be a Subsection. You'll have a visual of the data point and 500–750 words of written analysis about why this phenomenon may be happening, a client anecdote that illustrates the data point, a quote from an open-ended response that applies to the data point, and other secondary research of things happening in the world or industry that may be impacting the data point.

You'll want to map out your themes and data points (Sections and Subsections) before you put pen to paper on anything.

Important note: You'll need to pull out your keyword research here as well. Are there search terms you already found that are commonly used that naturally fit within your Sections and Subsections? Once you've mapped out your themes and data points, find at least one search term that best fits each. This will be important for titling the sections, and when we're breaking down each piece into Gold Bar Content.

Beyond the Sections and Subsections, other areas to include in your research report include:

- **Cover:** This will include your title and subtitle, plus your name, logo and website.

- **Executive summary:** 500 words sharing a broad overview of the findings, citing a few key data points.

- **Introduction:**

- **Section Dividers:** At the beginning of each Section, have a divider page with the Section title and 100–250 words about the theme and the general findings.

- **Conclusion:** 500-word recap of what the reader learned, why it was important, and what they should do with the information. You can also pull a client story or anecdote in here.

- **About the Author:** Your Brand Origin Story!

- **Next Steps:** This is the call-to-action for the Content Goldmine. It's a whole page dedicated to telling the reader how they can work with you (See the eBook section in this chapter for how the Next Steps page should look).

Once your Report is written and proofread, it's time to turn it over to a qualified, talented and proven designer who has experience with data visualization. You can look on sites like Fiverr or 99 Designs, but I highly encourage you to get recommendations from colleagues you trust. The way data is presented visually is too important to give this task to just anyone.

CHAPTER 5 - **SUMMARY**

- *Select your Content Goldmine topic by mapping out your content sweet spot—where what your prospects care about overlaps with what you offer*

- *When titling your Content Goldmine, focus on the search terms that relate to your topic and have high volume and low competition.*

- *For your Content Goldmine format, I recommend an eBook or Original Research Report for your first time out.*

- *If you already have a book written, a podcast going, or a course launched, these could act as your Content Goldmine.*

- *Map out the Chapters and Sections of your eBook before writing anything.*

- *If you outsource your Content Goldmine, be sure to provide the Chapter and Section map, as well as a solid overview about your brand messaging strategy.*

NOTES

CHAPTER 6:
Breaking Down Your Gold Bar Content

Take a breath. You're through the bulk of the work. With a completed Content Goldmine, you're ready to repurpose, preschedule, and optimize your way to content volume, quality and consistency.

And the best part? Every word that you publish has inherent value to your Best. Client. Ever because it comes from your Content Goldmine. And that bad boy was built just to provide value and solve problems for the people you care most about.

Ready to mine some Gold Bar Content? Let's do it!

What is Gold Bar Content?

Once you've completed your Content Goldmine—whether you've outsourced it or done it yourself—more than half the battle is done. Seriously. That's the hard part. Your next step is to break down your Content Goldmine into Gold Bar Content.

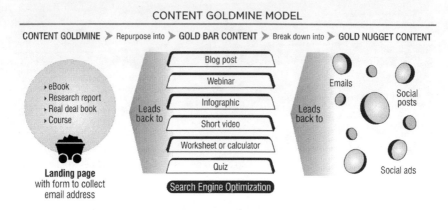

CONTENT GOLDMINE MODEL

Gold Bar Content is smaller, but still substantive content pieces that are perfect to act as weekly Star Content in your social media calendar. They're really the spine of your entire content program. They run the length of the year, providing consistency and structure for all the Gold Nuggets that are to come.

If you're in the mood to mix metaphors, if the Content Goldmine is a buffet, then your Gold Bar Content is the plate of food you get at the buffet. The Gold Nuggets are each bite that you take.

.When we talk about Gold Bar Content, we're really looking at 5 potential formats:

- Blog posts

- Mid-length videos (3–7 minutes)

- Webinars

- Infographics

- Short downloadable PDFs (sometimes called lead magnets)

Each of these types of Gold Bar Content has different conventions and expectations. You don't have to include all types. In fact, if blog posts or videos was the only type of Gold Bar Content you ever used, and you created them weekly as advised, you'd have a very solid content marketing program to build your credibility as an expert, create a following, and start getting known for your unique nerd zone. Mixing it up is purely extra credit.

For example, what if blog posts were your Gold Bar bread and butter, but you also did a webinar a few times a year? That would allow you some significant infusions of new email addresses into your list, and provide a nice platform from which to launch new products or offerings.

Or perhaps videos are your bread and butter, but you make it a point to do a quick downloadable PDF every month to make sure you have a consistent flow of new email addresses.

There are multiple ways to assemble Gold Bar Content types and there is plenty of room for innovation. The key thing to remember, however, is that you have two primary, non-negotiable goals for your Gold Bar Content:

1. Relentless consistency

2. Effective list-building

Everything else—novelty, innovation, breaking up the monotony of doing the same type of Gold Bar Content all the time—comes second to these critical goals. The entire point of the Content Goldmine model is to give you the consistency of volume that larger organizations use to be successful without the resources to hire it out to an agency or staff up a full marketing department. So breaking down that Goldmine for consistency is a must.

The good news is this: because you've already created your Content Goldmine, you don't have to worry about creating new content every week. There are two much easier, more proactive ways to prep your Gold Bar Content without having to set aside time to do it each week.

Prescheduling

Blogging and small lead magnets, in particular, lend themselves nicely to prescheduling. Once your Content Goldmine is finished, you can immediately turn each of your Sections or Subsections into stand-alone blog posts. Simply optimize each as outlined in the Blogging section below, and schedule for the week you want it to go live. If you want, you can schedule out a full year from your Content Goldmine by copying, pasting, and optimizing over the course of one afternoon. Or, you can break it up by half the year or quarter.

Small lead magnets are much the same. If you have multiple worksheets within your Content Goldmine, you can plan to make each of those available as a stand-alone lead magnet. Simply build out a blog post where you'll make those lead magnets available, add the email collection form, and schedule the date you want that page to go live. As with blog posts, you can do this for every worksheet in your Content Goldmine in a single afternoon. So let's say you have six worksheets in your Content Goldmine. You schedule one to go live for download every other month. Bam: you have a full year of small lead magnets ready to go.

Batching

When you already know which Gold Bar Content you're going to create ahead of time (and you should—it all already lives in your Content Goldmine), it is far more efficient to produce this repurposed content in batches.

If video is your primary Gold Bar Content type, you'll want to use your Content Goldmine text to create scripts for 6–12 videos at a time. Shoot them all at once, edit them all at once, upload them all at once, and be done with it. You can do this all in one day and avoid the painful context switching that always happens when you're trying to shoot, edit, upload and optimize a new video every week.

For infographics, if you've already had the data points of your Content Goldmine professionally designed and you're really happy with the data visualization they've provided, you have a couple of options. You can go back to the same designer and say, "Hey, can you make me six downloadable infographics from these data points you've already designed out? Here's the copy for each, and here are the data points I want you to include on each." It doesn't get much easier than that.

Or, if you're feeling all DIY about it, just snag the individual images of each data point, head into Canva and assemble your own infographics. Again, this is a task you'll want to batch. Once you complete one infographic, you can copy that file and use it as a template to create the rest. Once you get into a rhythm, this will go much faster if you dedicate a few hours to getting them all done than if you try to do them individually regularly.

Webinars are the one type of Gold Bar Content that batching and prescheduling don't really work for. I would say that webinars are the biggest, meatiest of the Gold Bar Content-type. They require presentation building, scripting, building the webinar on the actual platform you'll be using, and special promotional considerations. It's a bit more effort, but live webinars are still an incredibly powerful way to drive new ideal clients into your list.

Blogging

Where do you get your blog post content?

That's the easy part. If you created an eBook, each of these has the potential to be a stand-alone blog post:

- Section
- Intro
- Conclusion
- About the author

So if your eBook has 8 chapters, and each chapter has 6 sections, you're looking at 48 potential stand-alone blog posts. Add the intro, conclusion and about the author sections and you have 51 blog posts – enough for a full year of weekly posts.

If you created an original research report, each of these has the potential to be a stand-alone blog post:

- Each data point subsection
- Section overviews
- Executive summary
- Conclusion
- About the author

You're starting to see how this works, right? You are essentially copying and pasting these Sections that you've already created to make your blog posts. You then optimize them, schedule them for when you want them to go live, and boom: full year of blog content.

A question that I frequently get about this approach is if prospects can get all of this information in blog posts, why would they bother providing their email addresses to get the full

Content Goldmine? I have a few answers. First of all, have you ever known anyone willing to wait a year for anything when they can have it all immediately? An email address is such a low barrier to entry that no one would be willing to wait a full year to collect all of the information you'll be providing.

Second, they don't know that you're sharing all of the Content Goldmine information via your blog posts. You haven't shared your strategy with them. They haven't yet seen the Content Goldmine. And I don't care how smart and clever you are, no one is going to read ALL of your blog posts. The one or two that they do read gives them enough of a taste of the quality of information available in the full Content Goldmine. If they're interested in that much, they'll be interested in more.

Creating compelling blog headlines

Every blog post needs a headline that will make readers want to get in and take a closer look. There are two things that make a blog headline compelling:

1. It's structured in a way that is aligned with how people actually search

2. It creates curiosity

Ideally, your headline will do both. Either way, your headline must contain the most critical search term that your Best. Client. Ever! is looking for. You already know what this is—you built your Content Goldmine, and each of its Chapters and Sections around this.

As much as the creation of blog headlines seems like it should be a creative endeavor, it's disappointing to some (and a relief to others) that this is a highly formulaic process. Thanks to the fact that digital content is highly measurable, we've been able to determine over the last 20 years that there are a handful of blog headlines that always perform well. What can I say? Humans are predictable.

Here are 13 blog headline structures that are always successful. Just insert your search terms and you're off to the races:

1. The best way to _____.

2. The easiest way to _____.

3. The quickest/fastest way to _____.

4. Why you should _____.

5. What to do when _____.

6. Why X people do X thing (For example: Why Dr. Oz doesn't let his kids eat wheat and why you shouldn't either. Why Meryl Streep thinks Method Acting is a joke. Why successful executives use multiple headhunters. Why the wealthy delegate their money management.)

7. What I learned about _____ by being a _____. (For example: What I learned about parent-child dynamics by being a Kindergarten teacher, What I learned about financial planning as a pizza chef.)

8. # ways/ideas to _____.

9. # of mistakes that (insert dire consequence associated with search term) _____.

10. Everything you need to know about _____.

11. X vs. Y: Which is best for _____?

12. Counterintuitive claim: Why _____ will help you (result) _____. (For example: Why studying less will get you better grades, why eating more will help you lose weight, why talking less will improve communication with your kids,) These are particularly good choices if you've done an Original Research Report and found something surprising in your data.

13. #statistics about _____. (Another great one for those who've done Original Research Reports. People literally search for statistics by typing "stats about _____." Even if you haven't done a Research Report,

you can compile and cite secondary research stats on a topic in one place to meet the needs of searchers.)

Chances are you're looking at that list of headlines remembering times you clicked on blogs that were structured similarly. Sometimes the content delivered on the promise, sometimes it didn't. What makes you different is that your content comes from an expert perspective. It has inherent value to your Best. Client. Ever! Your blog content will pay off on the headline's promise.

Optimizing and activating your blog posts

Creating your blog title (also referred to in your content management system as your H1 tag) around your search term is the single most important thing you can do to optimize for search. This is the most important piece of text on the page as far as the search engine is concerned. So check that off your list.

There are three other areas you'll want to optimize for search, and neither will take long.

1. **Page title:** Most content management systems will take your blog title and make that the default page title. The page title is what shows up at the top of your web browser when you're on the page, and is the headline on the Google Search Engine Results Page (SERP) when your page shows up there. You'll want to adjust your page title slightly so it says:

   Blog Headline | Your Company Name | Search Term

2. **Page description/meta-description:** Different content management systems call this area different things. This is the text that shows up on the Google SERP below the title to tell you what the page or post is all about. You'll want to provide an accurate description of the blog post here that includes your core search term. Bonus points if you include language about who the blog post is for

(overscheduled moms on the go, procurement professionals seeking IT options, etc.)

3. **Image alt text:** If you have images in your blog post, please be sure to add "Alt text" in your content management system (Wordpress, Wix, Squarespace, etc.) The alt text is how the search engines (and programs that read web pages to visually impaired users) read the images. In the alt text field, provide a description of what the image shows, including the search terms.

That's it for search optimization. Now let's talk about optimizing your blog post for the human reader.

1. **Word count:** Despite the belief that less is more when it comes to reading, the research is clear. Blog posts under 500 words perform poorly. They're too short to provide any real value. Your sweet spot for word count is between 750-1,500 words, with 1,200 being ideal. The key is to keep the text skim-able using the next three ideas on this list.

2. **Subheads:** Break up your blog post with bold subheads that describe what the reader can expect in each subhead.

3. **Bulleted lists:** Bulleted lists help break up long areas of text and provide information in a digestible way.

4. **Images:** While every blog post should have a featured image at the top, add other images throughout that illustrate your point. It breaks up the text and makes the experience richer.

5. **Pull quotes:** Take particularly insightful bits of the blog post and format them as quotes (most content management systems apply special styling to quotes). The pull quote will appear in larger, stylized text that breaks up the article and provides guidance on what the reader should take away from the piece.

Now onto activation. One of the core tenants of the Content Goldmine model is infusing every piece of content (Gold Bar Content, Gold Nuggets, all of it) with action that takes your Best. Client. Ever! deeper into your content ecosystem. That means every one of your blog posts needs a call to action . . . or two or three.

End-of-post call to action: One required, non-negotiable tactic is a standardized call to action at the end of the blog post. This should include a subhead, short paragraph, and a clickable button that takes the reader where you want them to go. Example:

Want to know more about flipping houses?
Download the Ultimate Guide to Flipping Houses now to learn how to find, finance, buy, rehab, and sell properties. (Download now button)

Please note that the button doesn't say "Click here." It tells them the exact action that you want the reader to take. This button would link to the landing page where readers can access the Content Goldmine. Other calls to action could include linking to a webinar that you have available, to a landing page to download a small lead magnet, or to your calendar software to book an appointment with you. The key is that wherever you lead them from here should be a tactic that collects another email address.

In-post text link calls to action: Another call to action option on your blog post is adding simple text links throughout the blog post. These can link to other blog posts or two gated tactics like your Content Goldmine landing page, webinar registration, or other lead magnet landing pages. Not only are search engines big fans of internal links that take you to other areas of your own site, but it's great for the user experience too.

Sidebar text links: If your content management system is set up for you to easily create a sidebar on your blog posts, this is a great feature to take advantage of. You can build an image for this in Canva, then link the image to the destination page. As with the end-of-post call to action, you'll want this one to link to a piece of content that collects an email address—either your Content Goldmine landing page, a lead magnet page, a webinar registration page, or your appointment booking page.

Videos

Creating medium-length videos as your Gold Bar Content is a fantastic option if writing is just not your favorite. You can use the videos themselves across multiple platforms—including embedding them into blog posts or even just creating a blog post that houses the video, a brief text description of the video, and a call to action to a piece of gated content.

As I mentioned earlier in this chapter, the easiest way to produce videos is in batches. Create multiple scripts at once, shoot them in one go (so you only have to set up once), batch edit them, and batch upload them.

Medium-length videos should be between three and seven minutes long. You may have heard that your goal is to keep all videos under 90 seconds. Because this is Gold Bar Content, however, there's an expectation from your audience of some substance. They've clicked through to watch this video because they have a genuine interest in the topic and expect to learn something. Don't sell them short by trying to trim your video down to a too-short length. The 90-second guideline is more meant for promo-type videos, or videos that people don't self-select because they actually care about the content.

Video production

Every video project starts with a script. Use the Sections and Subsections of your Content Goldmine as the basis of your script. Run through it and make some edits to make it sound more conversational and natural, and consider restructuring your content to fit this script format:

1. Tell me who you are.

2. Tell me what you're going to share with me.

3. Tell me why I need it.

4. OK, now tell me the thing you want to tell me! (This is the meat.)

5. Tell me what to do next.

An example of how this plays out in a short video:

> Hey, it's Mary Kate, and I have a simple trick for creating webinars that could save you boatloads of time when you're getting ready to launch your next big one.
>
> Instead of starting with your slide deck, start with your talking points. Nail down the top five points that you really need to get across and figure out what you want to say on each of them. From there, develop visuals that support what you want to say, instead of just explaining what's on the screen (which is, after all, the most BORING way to do a webinar). Now that I go talking points first, it takes me about half the time to build out my webinar content.
>
> Want to see how I do it? Click the link in the description to get my free webinar talking points template, with tons of examples.

See how that works?

1. Tell me who you are: Mary Kate.

2. Tell me what you're going to share with me: A simple trick for creating webinars.

3. Tell me why I need it: It will save you boatloads of time.

4. OK, now tell me the thing: That whole second paragraph.

5. Tell me what to do next: Click the link in the description to get the template.

Your meaty info section will likely be longer than this example, but you get the idea.

Decide if your video is just going to be you talking to the camera (face-to-camera style), you sharing a slide deck with your face narrating in the corner (using Loom or similar software), or some sort of tutorial or screen-share. If it's anything more than just face-to-camera, you'll want to plan out the visual elements (the slide deck, the screen share, what you'll be doing in the tutorial, etc.).

If you will be filming yourself or another human subject, you'll want to keep your studio set-up simple, and focus most of your attention on audio and lighting.

Audio: I recommend the Rode SmartLav. You can hook it directly into your smartphone, which is an excellent video camera. If you're using a DSLR or more advanced camera, you can hook your SmartLav into your phone to record the audio, then synch the audio and video up in post-production. Or, you can purchase a wireless lav mic so the audio connects directly to your camera.

Lighting: A ring light or soft box can do the trick. Better yet, if you're filming in a room with a lot of natural light, just make sure you're facing a window when you shoot. If you have to use an artificial lighting source, I prefer a soft box light to a ring light, because the rings can make you look a little zombie-like. No matter what you use, you want all the light shining evenly across your face to avoid creating shadows. Light from above causes shadows below, light from below causes shadows above (remember holding a flashlight under your chin and telling ghost stories when you were a kid? That's not the look we're going for).

Tripod: Whatever you're using for your camera, you'll want to spring for a tripod that works with it. This will ensure that you can shoot from the angle you want (just a bit above the face tilted slightly down) and avoid camera shake. Many of my first videos have my then8-year-old holding my DSLR. You can imagine how attractive that angle was.

Teleprompter: For scripted face-to-camera videos, a teleprompter is essential. What is also essential is that the teleprompter is positioned in such a way that it appears you are looking into the camera. You can purchase teleprompter boxes that work with a tablet and affix to your tripod so that it appears that you're looking directly into the lens while reading. A scrappier fix? Use a free teleprompter app (there are dozens of them) on your tablet or smartphone that runs the script while you're recording so you can read the script while looking right at the camera.

Video editing and hosting

Everyone has different preferences for doing their own video editing. I tend to do most of mine in iMovie, but I know many coaches, consultants and solopreneurs who swear by Camtasia. Either way, you'll need to learn a bit about editing if you're going to do it yourself. And editing video can be tedious and time-consuming.

I'm a big fan of Fiverr for video editing. It's cheap and easy to upload your video and a few editing notes (Do you want your name to appear in the lower third? Do you want a call to action on screen at the end? Which time-stamped segments of your raw video footage do you want to include? Do you want them to minimize any background noise)? The turnaround time is usually quick and if what you want is not too complicated, you typically get what you ask for without wasting a ton of time on editing.

For hosting your videos, YouTube is still the go-to. If you want greater security, like if you're using videos for courses and you don't want everyone to have access to them, Vimeo is a better choice. Vimeo also has functionality allows you to create short videos for social media, which is a nice addition. Either way, if you want your videos to be publicly available and easy to find via a search on either of these platforms, you'll want to take a few minutes to optimize each video.

Optimization for YouTube

YouTube is not only the most popular video hosting platform in the world, but it's also the second most popular search engine. As video drives more views across all platforms, a solid understanding of how to do things right on the 'Tube will make sure your efforts get the attention they deserve.

Channel Branding

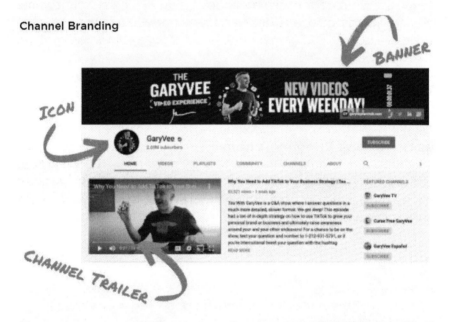

When it comes to branding your channel, the first places to look are the icon and the banner. The ICON represents you. While large brands will often use their logo as the icon, I recommend personal brands, coaches and professional service businesses to use their face.

The BANNER tells visitors what your channel is about and why they should subscribe. I recommend using this space to share your upload schedule or Content Mission Statement, in addition to a great photo of yourself and your company's logo.

Next, and often overlooked, is your CHANNEL TRAILER. You can set a different channel trailer for subscribers and new visitors. I recommend having a "what you're about" video for new visitors, and your latest upload for subscribers.

Video branding

CUSTOM THUMBNAILS don't only make a significant impact on the professionalism of your visual branding, they also affect the search ranking of your videos and how frequently they're chosen from the SERP. I recommend a custom thumbnail for every video that includes text telling the user what to expect.

Within YouTube Studio, in the video editor, you have the option to add an END SCREEN. While an End Screen can be used to reinforce your visual brand, you'll find that you don't have many action options if you're not yet a YouTube Partner Program member. You will only be able to use your End Screen to link to another of your channels, recommend next videos, and request to subscribe. In your early stages, I recommend pushing for the subscribe, and recommending two videos: your most recent, and the "best for the viewer" dynamic option.

Calls to action

Aside from End Screens, the only in-video CTAs available within YouTube are CARDS. And like End Screens, if you're not part of the YouTube Partner Program, their functionality is limited. You can use up to five Cards per video to link to other videos, playlists or channels.

The most valuable place to house calls to action for beginners is in your video descriptions and in the ABOUT tab of your channel. Not only is it an ideal place to tell your brand story, but you can also link to your website, freebie landing pages, other social media profiles—whatever. The About area is also a prime area to optimize with your most critical search terms.

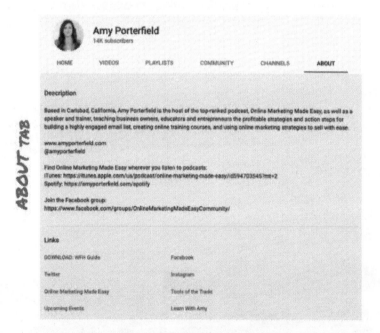

Optimization of videos for YouTube search

When uploading a video, there are multiple places to make sure you're optimizing. Use this as a way to make sure you're hitting them all, and include your most critical keywords in these spots.

- Video title

- Video description

- Spoken word—make sure you SAY each video's relevant search term

- Tags—include all relevant keywords

- Custom thumbnail text—you can create a custom thumbnail in Canva that includes the video's title right on the screen

- Captions/Subtitles (SRT file): You can submit your videos to Rev.com to get quick-turnaround caption files in just a few hours for just a few dollars. And if you plan to share videos on social media, this is a must-do, no matter what platform you're using.

Optimizing videos for social media

Generally, a medium-form video is not the appropriate length for any of the social platforms (except possibly LinkedIn). If you're planning to share the videos on the social platforms, you'll want a shorter, teaser version that links to your larger video.

When sharing videos via social media, ALL major platform algorithms favor native video content over video content on other platforms. Put simply, all social platforms will show your video to more people when you upload it directly. If you link to YouTube or Vimeo, fewer people will see your post. You'll also want to add the SRT file so that your video on social has captions. Most viewers will see your video on auto-play on their mobile devices, and the sound won't be enabled. With captions, they'll still be able to watch and learn from you without actually clicking the video to enable the sound.

All the major social platforms also give greater priority to livestream videos than pre-recorded videos. So if you want to promote a video on another platform, I recommend using a livestream video to do so. That way, you don't need to edit and optimize another finished video to upload. You can just jump on live, tell them what your video is about, provide a link, and be out. Livestreams also don't have the same length norms as pre-edited videos do on social media. People are totally fine with you yammering away for 5, 10 or 20 minutes. Just make sure your livestream length is proportionate to whatever video you're promoting. So . . . don't go live for 20 minutes to promote a 5-minute video.

Webinars

And now, we have reached the mother of all Gold Bar Content types. The big one. Live webinars require the most work . . . but they are also the best at generating email addresses. And when you're done, you have a replay that you can continue to use as a gated asset until the end of time. So that's nice.

Here's your to-do list for creating a webinar:

1. Choose a platform

2. Build your promotional plan

3. Create your deck

4. Create your reminder emails

5. Create your follow-up sequence

6. Build your landing page and social media promotions to drive registrations

7. Do the webinar!

8. Repurpose the replay

So, yeah, kind of a hefty to-do list. I don't recommend doing webinars more than once per quarter unless they're a core part of your sales strategy. It's just a lot of work and quite a bit of planning. The end result is usually worth it, but doing them too frequently will suck all your time and attention away from other areas of your business.

Your webinar can be built around a full chapter of your Content Goldmine, depending on what you want to cover. You'll want to keep the content relatively focused on one problem the attendees are looking to solve. All of the promotion for the webinar should be around how they solve that one problem.

Your platform

If you already have Kajabi or Clickfunnels, you'll find that you can conduct your webinar within these platforms. I don't think the functionality is the greatest, but if you're already paying for the resource, you might as well get your money's worth. And you don't need the world's greatest functionality if you're only doing one webinar per quarter.

If you don't already have a webinar platform, but you have a Zoom account, you may want to look into getting the webinar upgrade. You're already familiar with the platform, so this would be a nice easy transition.

If you're wanting something a little more robust, I really like WebinarJam and WebinarNinja. WebEx and GoToWebinar are good, but they're more enterprise-level solutions, so are often not affordable for small businesses. WebinarJam and WebinarNinja are both roughly the same cost, and they both have your registration page, thank you page, reminder emails, and basic follow-up emails built into the experience—making it much easier to get through that webinar to-do list.

No matter what you use, DO A PRACTICE RUN. Work with a friend and make sure that you know how to use all the display and chat functionalities within your platform. We can pretty much assume that something will go wrong with tech. The more familiar you are with the platform, the easier it will be to deal with it when it happens. As often as possible, have someone on the live webinar with you to field questions and troubleshoot tech issues.

Basic tips

When you're building out your slide deck, make sure you're not using a lot of fancy animations. Keep it simple—your face and your visuals on-screen. When you don't need a presentation to be showing, maximize your face so it feels more like a one-to-one conversation.

Use a pair of air buds or a USB mic for better sound quality. And for the love of all that is good in this universe, PLEASE make sure you have ample bandwidth. If possible, bust out an ethernet cable to ensure really good Internet. No one wants to see you all pixelated and hear you sounding like a robot.

Use your intro to tell an abbreviated version of your Brand Origin Story. Let people know why this topic is important to you. On a webinar, the audience is in it with you, experiencing what you're saying live. They've said they're interested in what you have to say and they've shown up to hear you say it. So tell them why it matters to you.

Keep the information portion of the webinar focused and highvalue. When you move into a sales pitch, let the people know that's what you're doing so they don't feel duped. If you want them to stay till the end, offer them an incentive for doing so, like a free download. But don't trick them into staying. That's Fake Guru strategy.

If you're using WebinarNinja, WebinarJam or any of the advanced webinar platforms, they'll automatically send out the replay to all registrants. You can also download the replay video, and put it behind an email form for future use to continue collecting email addresses.

Infographics

For those brave souls who have taken on the Original Research Report as your Content Goldmine, you'll want to look at the infographic as a definite Gold Bar Content tactic. These interesting data visualizations are captivating to look at, and position you as a thought leader who understands the data and issues facing your audience so well that you're able to do more than simply report on it.

Here are some examples of good infographics:

PET STATS & FACTS in the U.S.

Estimated Number of Pets in Homes:
83.3 Million
95.6 Million

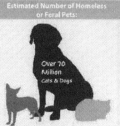

Estimated Number of Homeless or Feral Pets:
Over 70 Million Cats & Dogs

approximately
7.6 MILLION
pets enter shelters every year!

Pets Entering Shelters Yearly:
3.9 Million
3.4 Million

Pets Adopted Yearly:
1.4 Million
1.3 Million

Where Pet Owners Get Their Cats From:
- Friend or Family 41%
- Other 6%
- Bought 8%
- Adoption 20%
- Stray 22%

Where Pet Owners Get Their Dogs From:
- Bought 41%
- Friend or Family 38%
- Other 6%
- Adoption 28%

Pets Euthanized Yearly:
1.2 Million Dogs
1.4 Million Cats

PET OVERPOPULATION

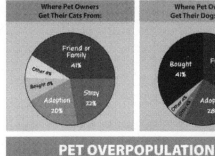

Puppies Per Litter: 6-10

Litters Possible Per Year: x2

One Dog & Her Offspring Could Produce 67,000 Dogs in 6 Years!

Kittens Per Litter: 4-6

Litters Possible Per Year: x3

One Cat & Her Offspring Could Produce 420,000 Cats in 7 Years!

More Than
55%
of pets entering shelters every year will never be adopted

WHY DO PEOPLE GIVE AWAY THEIR PETS?

- 29% Residence Doesn't Allow Pets
- 10% Not Enough Time
- 10% Divorce or Death
- 10% Behavior Issues

- 21% Residence Doesn't Allow Pets
- 11% Allergies

WHAT CAN I DO TO HELP?

Spay or neuter your pet - It costs less than raising puppies or kittens.

Keep your pets leashed or indoors so they can't run away or get lost.

Keeping an ID Tag on your pet's collar & having them microchipped can help get your pet safely home if they do become lost.

Consider Adopting Your Next Furry Family Member & Help Reduce The Number of Pets in Shelters!

Owned Pets Live Longer Healthier & Happier Lives!

Brought To You By thatpetplace.com

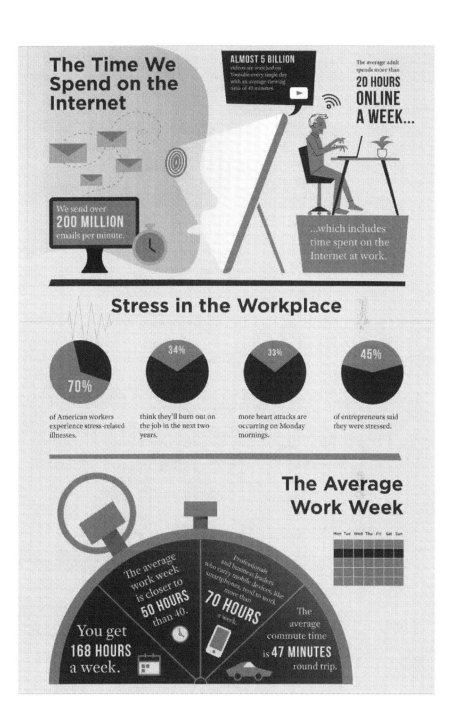

The Time We Spend on the Internet

ALMOST 5 BILLION videos are watched on Youtube every single day with an average viewing time of 40 minutes.

The average adult spends more than **20 HOURS ONLINE A WEEK...**

We send over **200 MILLION** emails per minute.

...which includes time spent on the Internet at work.

Stress in the Workplace

70% of American workers experience stress-related illnesses.

34% think they'll burn out on the job in the next two years.

33% more heart attacks are occurring on Monday mornings.

45% of entrepreneurs said they were stressed.

The Average Work Week

Mon Tue Wed Thu Fri Sat Sun

The average work week is closer to **50 HOURS** than 40.

Professionals and business leaders who carry mobile devices, like smartphones, tend to work more than **70 HOURS** a week.

The average commute time is **47 MINUTES** round trip.

You get **168 HOURS** a week.

As you can see, while an infographic is definitely sharing the data, it's much more about the visual experience. An effective infographic translates the data into something that users understand inherently by looking at it, so it's easier to internalize.

At this point, I feel compelled to reiterate my recommendation that if you're working with data visualization, that you bring on a designer to help you. While a great infographic is an incredibly powerful piece of content, a badly designed infographic is, at best, ignored and, at worst, ridiculed. In short, if you're going to do this, do it right!

If you're feeling extra scrappy and want to have a go at your own infographics, please don't try to build it in Canva. You'll have much better luck in a platform like Easelly or Visme, that's geared specifically to non-designers who want to build infographics.

If you plan on breaking down your Original Research Report into a series of infographics, consider breaking down each section into one infographic. Your sections are based on specific data themes, so in theory, all of the data points in one section should work together as part of a collection to tell one story.

You can even do one infographic to cover what's in your executive summary. This infographic would act as a sneak peek to the full Content Goldmine, and can be an excellent teaser to get interested users to opt-in to receive more information from you.

If your Content Goldmine is an eBook, you still may have some infographic potential. Think about creating a roadmap that shows the transformation a client goes through as they work through the eBook, or some other process infographic like a funnel or flow chart. This is a great way to tease the larger piece of content.

Infographics, in general, should be ungated content. That means that you don't require an email address to access them. Five years ago, I would have given you different advice, because users were willing to give up an email address for an infographic at that time. Now, however, this content format doesn't command an email address. They can, however, be interesting enough to get people to want to learn more.

Of course, every infographic should come with a call to action that pushes to the Content Goldmine. You can house your infographic as an image file within a blog post or landing page (so the call to action would be similar to what you use at the bottom of your blog posts), or as an image you upload to social media (and you'd put your call to action in the description).

And because your infographics are often image files (.png or .jpg extension), you'll want to include alt text with your important keywords.

Small Lead Magnets

Downloadable PDFs are great Gold Bar Content pieces for a few reasons. First of all, they're easy as pie to make. If your Content Goldmine already has worksheets or checklists included, you can just pull out any one of these and make it a downloadable asset. Even if you don't have these types of pages already created, popping into Canva or a quiz making app and creating your own is quick, simple and fun.

Second, outside of your Content Goldmine and webinars, this is the next best way to capture email addresses for your list. Because they're so easy to create, you can try multiple concepts to see what your audience responds most passionately to. It's easy to judge—just count the email addresses you collect.

Of all the options you can create for small lead magnets, these 10 are some of the most popular and consistently best performing:

1. Checklist
2. Budgeting worksheet

3. Workplan/schedule

4. Template they can follow to create their own

5. Audio downloads

6. Calculator

7. Cheat sheet (summary/list of facts they'll need to know)

8. Goal setting pages/structured prompts

9. Quizzes

10. Resource list

In order to capture an email address, your lead magnet will need to be accessed through a landing page. You can create a landing page in multiple ways. Most customer relationship management (CRM) systems/autoresponders—from basic ones like Mailchimp to high-end ones like Keap/Infusionsoft and HubSpot—will allow you to create a templated landing page with a lead-capture form to house your lead magnet. When your prospect completes the form on this page, they're directed to a Thank You page where they can access the PDF. You'll usually want to set up an email to immediately send the PDF to the new contact as well.

If you're using an autoresponder or website content management system that doesn't allow you to easily create landing page, you will want to work with a landing page provider like ClickFunnels or Leadpages. However, these are cost-prohibitive enough that it might just make sense to switch to a CRM that lets you do it all.

I highly recommend using your Thank You page (the page that users go to after they click "submit" on the landing page) to provide a strong call to action for what users should do next— whether that's scheduling a consult, signing up for a webinar, or purchasing a low-ticket product. You have their attention now— make use of it!

These freebies can easily be shared in the Facebook groups you've discovered that cater to your Best. Client. Ever! This is a powerful list-building strategy. If there are Facebook groups that you're active in that already serve your ideal client, many will have promotion days when you can share you free downloads. Even those groups that don't provide self-promotional opportunities, many of the members will have questions about your topic. Answer them. Provide value. Share expertise. And if you feel that one of your downloads might work for someone you're talking to, simply ask if they'd like a link. Easy peasy.

Naturally, you'll want to share the link to your landing page in your own Facebook group, or on whatever social platform you're focusing on.

CHAPTER 6 - **SUMMARY**

- *Gold Bar Content pieces are smaller than the Content Goldmine, but still substantive enough to drive traffic or warrant the prospect of providing an email address.*

- *Use any combination of Gold Bar Content types that allows you to publish consistently every week.*

- *Use sections or subsections of your Content Goldmine and turn them into blog posts. Just copy, paste, and make a few optimization tweaks.*

- *Medium-form educational videos can be made using the content of sections and subsections as the basis for your script. Reformat to tell viewers:*

  o *Who you are*

  o *What they can expect to learn*

  o *How they'll benefit*

  o *The actual content you want to tell them*

  o *What they should do next.*

- *Webinars are a powerful email collecting tool, but they're time-consuming so stick to about once each quarter maximum.*

- *Infographics are first and foremost a visual medium. If you're not prepared to hire a good designer to create these for you, don't bother.*

- *Small lead magnets are easy to create. Make sure you use a CRM/autoresponder that lets you easily standup landing pages.*

NOTES

Social Media Distribution: Gold Nuggets

Now we've got a Content Goldmine living behind a landing page gate, some blog posts and videos being awesome, and maybe a webinar registration page taking up some digital real estate. So how do we let people know about them?

We mined some Gold Nuggets. And we leave a trail of them across your social media platforms so your Best. Client. Ever! can find your expertise and more importantly, an expert like you to work with.

When you're an expert in a specific field but NOT an expert in social media, nothing is more frustrating than trying to figure out how to share that expertise in an effective way. You feel like you're being bombarded with platform after platform after platform, expected to understand the intricacies of each.

You find people using the word "algorithm" way too much for your taste.

And you're starting to think that these social media people are speaking in some made-up language that was designed specifically to make you feel dumb.

Well, you're partially right.

Social media and digital marketing gurus make their money by creating the impression that they know more than you do. That they're more tech-savvy than others. So their language is often intentionally . . . bullshitty, for lack of a better word. It's jargon stew. And it's OK if that drives you nuts.

The truth about social media platforms is that they're not actually that hard, because you rarely need to know EVERY LITTLE THING about them. You need to perform a few key functions. And those are the key functions you need to know how to do.

Hey, in some cases, you don't even need to know that. You just need to know the outcome you want to achieve, and you can have a virtual assistant or freelance digital marketing specialist do it for you. That's always an option.

But even if you are planning to outsource part or all of your social media management, I want you to know enough to formulate a strategy. That's something a smarty-pants like you can easily understand without ever hearing the word "algorithm."

What are Gold Nuggets?

In the Content Goldmine model that we're using to help you create the volume, frequency and quality of content you need to take ownership of your area of expertise online, Gold Nuggets are the smallest content unit. It's what we break down from the Content Goldmine and Gold Bar Content pieces for sharing across social media platforms. Emails live in the Gold Nugget category as well, but I've dedicated the entire next chapter to that.

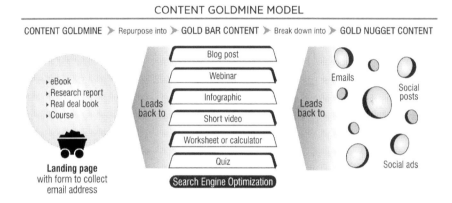

CONTENT GOLDMINE MODEL

CONTENT GOLDMINE ▷ Repurpose into ▷ GOLD BAR CONTENT ▷ Break down into ▷ GOLD NUGGET CONTENT

- eBook
- Research report
- Real deal book
- Course

Landing page
with form to collect
email address

Leads back to

Blog post
Webinar
Infographic
Short video
Worksheet or calculator
Quiz

Search Engine Optimization

Leads back to

Emails
Social posts
Social ads

And when I say, "sharing across social media platforms," let's be clear: I don't mean ALL social media platforms.

For your Minimum Viable Content Experience in Chapter 4, you started focusing on one social platform. Now that we're getting ready to start sharing your larger content ecosystem, we'll want to expand your reach across a whopping TWO platforms. Maximum.

Yeah, and truth be told, if you want to just stick with one platform, you can. Remember, the name of the game is consistency and sustainability. If you start with a plan to create a robust presence across all the major platforms, you won't consistently succeed on any of them. And that is not the kind of outcome we're interested in.

So take a look at the platform you selected for your Minimum Viable Content Experience. Unless that was an unmitigated disaster (and by definition, and MVCE cannot be an unmitigated disaster—it is all just learning), you'll want to stick with that platform.

If you're feeling like you want a little more, add one more platform. As before, you'll choose your platform based on two criteria:

1. Is your Best. Client. Ever! there, engaging with content in your area of expertise?

2. Do you have a baseline level or comfort with the platform, or a strong desire to learn it?

For that first criterion, please note that your audience should not only be there, but they should be there consuming content on your topic. Take me, for example. I spend a lot of time on LinkedIn. Primarily, I'm consuming content on the financial advice industry (because a lot of my clients fall in this category, and much of my professional life has revolved around supporting financial professionals) and digital marketing (because that's my jam). There may very well be information on LinkedIn about fitness, yoga, meditation, allergen-free cooking, or other topics that are important to my life, but I wouldn't know because I have no desire to consume that content there.

The same goes for Instagram. I'm there and I consume a lot of content about Paleo eating, coaching, mindset, etc. I would not be interested in consuming information about the financial industry on Instagram, because that's not why I'm there.

See my point? So where is your Best. Client. Ever! interested in consuming information about your topic? Here's a breakdown of the social media channels we'll discuss and how you would find your Best. Client. Ever!

LinkedIn: You're solving business problems for an ideal client that is a professional at a small or large business. This could be a business owner, but is not a solopreneur, and works in a more traditional vertical (such as finance, human resources, procurement/sourcing). These ideal clients will tend to be over the age of 30. The content they're consuming here is about the business they're in.

Instagram: If your ideal client is focused on visual, lifestyle or event-specific needs, and is under the age of 35, and is likely female. If you're a stylist, event planner, caterer, fitness or wellness professional focused on younger clients and you're comfortable producing highly visual content, IG is a good choice. The content they're consuming here is about their business if it's a coaching or marketing business, but otherwise, it's about their visually-focused hobbies.

Facebook: The old standby. If your ideal client is older than 35, a solopreneur or coach, a small business owner, OR you just don't feel like you have a great handle on your ideal client's demographics, this is where you want to start. People on Facebook are consuming news content, content about their business (if they're a solopreneur). They use Facebook Groups focused on their business verticals.

Twitter: This is the right choice for very few experts, coaches or consultants who have a specific niche to serve. That said, if your ideal client is focused on technology-oriented business or traditional media, you can start here. People on Twitter are there to see opinions, follow influencers in their industry, and comment on news in their industry.

Pinterest: This wasn't included in the original set of social platform options for a number of reasons I'll discuss in the Pinterest section. Pinterest is a platform that is adopted primarily by women who are looking for lifestyle-related educational content—style, cooking, fitness, solopreneurship, parenting, relationships, etc. It is an incredibly powerful platform if your business fits into this category.

NOTE: You'll notice that I'm not discussing Snapchat or TikTok. There's a reason for this. Snapchat's functionality has been replicated by Instagram Stories, leaving the platform slim pickings for expert content. While there are plenty of people over the age of 30 using Snapchat, they're not there for consumer helpful content. They're there for fun. At the time of publication, TikTok is in danger of being banned by US users. It is also too new for widespread adoption and norms to take hold of people using the platform for educational or expert content. Instagram Reels is attempting to replicate the TikTok experience, so it's possible that Zuck's #2 platform will take TikTok's place. If it doesn't, and TikTok becomes a mainstay of the social landscape, I'll be keeping an eye on it and how experts and content consumers use the platform to find each other.

Facebook

With 2.45 billion (with a freaking 'b') active monthly users, Facebook is still the biggest and most commanding of all the social media platforms. Growing most rapidly among older audiences, Facebook is a legacy platform in a world of more innovative competitors who appeal more to younger audiences.

Use of Facebook among older generations is rising rapidly

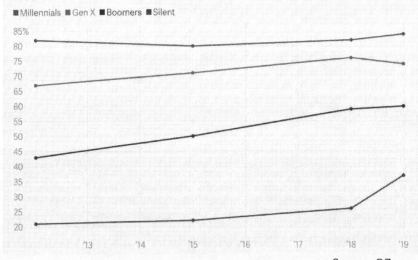

Source: QZ.com

YouTube, Instagram and Snapchat are the most popular online platforms among teens

% of U.S. teens who say ...

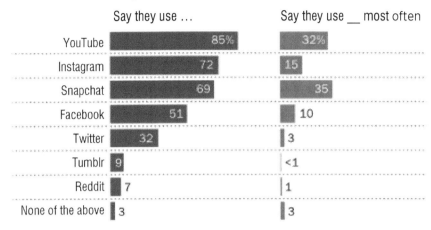

Note: Figures in first column add up to more than 100% because multiple responses were allowed. Question about most-used site was asked only of respondents who use multiple sites; results have been recalculated to include those who only use one site. Respondents who did not give an answer are not shown.

Source: Survey conducted March 7-April 10, 2018.
Teens, Social Media & Technology 2018

PEW RESEARCH CENTER

Facebook is also an optimal platform if you have an international audience. Only 10% of Facebook users reside in the US or Canada. By contrast, a whopping 41.3% of users are from the Asia-Pacific region according to the company's Q3 2019 earnings presentation.

In the US, the platform skews female, and 74% of users are high-income earners and college graduates. In short, it's a great platform for selling high-ticket coaching and consulting offerings.

If you've determined that Facebook is your platform of choice, let's talk about how to best use what Zuckerberg has created for you to best promote your expertise, generate leads, and grow your business.

Business Pages vs. Profiles vs. Groups

Before we discuss anything else, I want to make the clear point that not every posting option on Facebook is created equal. From the beginning of the platform, businesses have been pushed to create Facebook Business Pages and push their "fans" to follow them there. So that's just what we did.

And that's when the trap was sprung.

Between 2014 and 2018, Facebook rolled out a number of algorithm changes that effectively eliminated the ability for businesses to reach their followers organically using their business pages. You wanted eyeballs on your business page content? You had to buy ads.

A study from Social@Ogilvy, a major social media agency, shows that organic reach on Business Pages dropped from 16% in February 2012 to 6.5% in March of 2014. By 2016, organic reach on Business pages dropped less than 2%.

Sure, these changes were all under the auspices of providing more of what consumers wanted—quality content that focused on their interests and connections—but you don't have to be a genius to figure out that the 'Book was making on-platform ad spend a non-negotiable for small businesses who wanted to increase their reach.

In January 2018, Facebook's Head of News Feed, Adam Mosseri announced that the latest algorithm update would "shift ranking to make News Feed more about connecting with people and less about consuming media in isolation." That's the whole point of social media, right?

But the result wasn't amazing for small businesses, solopreneurs, and experts who had spent the previous years building a following to their business pages.

So marketers had to start getting creative.

Even though Facebook generally frowns on using your personal profile for business, what you're building is a personal brand. Getting consistent engagement with posts from your personal profile will get far more organic reach than from a business page. And if you have an active group? Those posts will take you even further. Facebook has publicly committed and continues to reinforce its interest in growing engagement in Groups.

And it makes sense. I can't count the people I've talked to in the last two years who have said, "I'm only on Facebook for the groups." There's a boatload of power here, as it seems that Group content will continue to be prioritized.

So the TLDR on this? Your Facebook business page has only 2 purposes: to act as your on-platform digital storefront that houses information about your business, and to run ads. A post on your Business Page every now and then is fine, but it is the least relevant property on Facebook when it comes to finding new followers with free traffic.

Making your posts as powerful as possible

Whether you're posting on your personal profile, in a Group (yours or someone else's), or from your business page, there are certain parameters you want to stick to in order to ensure your post gets all the organic eyeballs possible.

1. Go live: Facebook is prioritizing video and live video as a matter of corporate strategy. Live videos get 6x more engagement than pre-recorded videos, and engagement gets you . . . wait for it . . . more views and engagement!

2. Post with the intent to get people talking: Ask questions, ask for action, but use your posts to generate engagement. Reactions (angry faces, hearts, tears) get more weight than simple "Likes," and comments and link clicks are weighted more heavily still. Tell people what you want them to do!

3. Post often and consistently: The more consistently and often you post, the more value you can provide to your audience, the more engagement you create with yourself as a publisher, and the more likely your audience is to be served up your future posts.

4. Timing: Post when your audience is on the platform. You can use a social media management tool (Hootsuite, Buffer, Planoly, SmarterQueue, etc.) to schedule your posts for certain times across all platforms or the Facebook Creator Studio on your Business Page. Hootsuite data reveals that B2B content performs better on Tuesday, Wednesday and Thursday between 9 am–2 pm. B2C content performs best around noon on Monday, Tuesday and Wednesday.

5. Don't be your paranoid Uncle Mike: You know, that relative that we all have who is constantly posting conspiracy theories and links to fringe news sites? Facebook has brought the hammer down on Fake News, so this should go without saying, but don't be that guy.

Optimizing your personal profile page

On your profile page, you can't really do any selling. In the past, businesses would use their personal page to push people to their Business Page. Well, we've talked about how futile that is. So think about what you will want your followers to do. What is the hub of your content?

- Will you want them to join your Facebook Group? Then build your cover photo, bio, and large image area around this call to action.

- Will your posts be sending them to your website a lot? To read blog posts, access freebies? Then make sure your cover image, bio and large image area are sending them to that site.

Groups

I know I just told you that Facebook Groups are extremely powerful. And they are. But I also want to warn you that building an effective group that's well populated and active and engaged is a LOT of work.

- Initial content: In the beginning, you'll be posting multiple times a day, and you'll be the only one posting. There will be zero engagement, and you'll have very few joiners.

- Getting new members: You'll want to be hanging out in other Facebook Groups that serve your audiences, providing value to people who have questions, posting helpful content. For those who interact with you in these Groups, invite them to join yours. Make friends with ideal clients, and as you DM them to learn more about them, ask if they're interested in joining your group. ONLY IF THEY SAY THEY ARE, you can send them a link to join.

- Providing value: You'll want to broker partnerships with other experts who serve your audience to provide guest content (Live trainings are best) in the group to drive more traffic in. You'll want to run challenges.

If you have a group, get familiar with the tools Facebook offers for group admins. You can schedule posts in the group, insights to learn more about the makeup of your group and how they're interacting, units to provide ongoing learning, events and watch parties to create synchronous experiences, and more. There's more functionality being added here all the time to help your group thrive.

Like I said, it's a lot of work. But even a small and active group will grow over time if you're consistent, continue adding value, and actively recruit new members. And it's a fantastic platform to launch new products to, test new offerings, and get amazing customer feedback.

I would recommend getting your message and content figured out before starting a group. Starting a group without a solid content plan is just asking for a ghost-town experience that makes you feel like a failure. Harsh, but super true.

Optimizing your Business Page

Now that we've established the limited role that a Facebook Business Page should play in your social media plan, let's talk about how to make the best use of it. One of the two key reasons to use a Business Page is so it can act as the on-platform home for all information about your business.

- Choose the right name: If your business doesn't have a name beyond yours, shoot for something with this format—"First LastName—What I do, "For example, my Business Page is Mary Kate Gulick—Content Marketing Coach. If your business does have a name, you may still want to get your personal name in there somewhere because in most cases, people will be coming to your page because they know you. This might be something like "Business Name with First LastName." Consider something like Xtreme Bookkeeping with Brian Jones or Transformations Coaching with Julie Marshall.

- Choose the right template. Facebook offers multiple pre-made business page templates that offer features that are appropriate for your type of business. If you're building a consulting, coaching or other professional services practice, you want the "Business" template.

- Choose the right call to action—there's an option to add a page button on your Business Page. This should be the one primary thing you want visitors to do. Is it to book an appointment with you? Choose the booking button. To go to your website? Choose that button. To join your group? You get the idea.

- Add a custom URL in the settings area, so you can be facebook.com/yourcompany instead of facebook.com/random numbers.

- Complete your description area using your Bite-Sized Brand Bio and Brand Origin Story.

- Add your website.

- If you have packaged services or offerings, you can add those as well.

- Enable reviews and ask new clients to provide reviews here.

- Don't forget those visuals: Your profile pic can be your logo or a picture of you. Your cover image should promote the most important program at the moment. That could be something you're selling, joining your group, downloading your lead magnet, whatever. This real estate should be dedicated to your current priority.

Posts vs. Stories

There are currently two ways to post organic content on Facebook—posts that are viewed in the newsfeed and Stories that show up in the Stories section. Stories area a functionality that originated on Snapchat, where the content disappears after 24 hours. It made its way to Instagram first, and when Stories showed they could be successful on other platforms, Zuck brought it to Facebook.

Currently, Facebook Stories has more than 300 million active daily users. Stories can accommodate video and images. Because the dimensions of Stories are so different, if you want to be in stories, you'll find yourself creating story-specific content. In the spirit of keeping things simple, I generally recommend that solopreneurs who are just trying to build a consistent presence stick to the posts until it becomes second nature. At that point, you can branch into Stories.

Video and Facebook Live

Unlike participating in Stories, video and Facebook Live are non-negotiables. The company has already said it's leaning in (see what I did there?) to video and plan to be a primarily video platform over the coming years. As such, the algorithm favors video over any other type of content, and favors Live video over other types of video.

For pre-recorded videos, it's critical that you have them captioned. You can do this by submitting your video to a captioning site such as Rev.com and paying a few bucks for a .SRT file. Once you receive your file, simply upload the video, click "Edit Video" and upload the .SRT file in the captions section. Easy peasy. We do this because most interaction on Facebook happens on mobile devices, and most mobile devices auto-play videos with no sound. If you require users to turn on the sound in order to get your message, you will miss most of them.

While conventional wisdom has always told us that short video is better for social media, Facebook is favoring high-quality video content that goes beyond the 3-minute mark. So in short, make your videos count. If you're going to go live or create a pre-produced video, have some high-value meat in it. Your Content Goldmine should be a massive help here.

Boosted posts and Facebook ads

I like to start all discussions about paid social media with this point. Don't do it until you completely nail down your message and have figured out what's working organically. Otherwise, you're just throwing money after an unknown. The purpose of putting money behind a message on Facebook is to get more eyeballs on a message that you already know to be effective. Too many personal brands, coaches and consultants have just poured money into Facebook ads without understanding what message works for their audience.

Now that we have that out of the way, let's talk about the difference between boosted posts and Facebook ads. Both are only available on your Facebook Business Page. While Facebook considers both of them "ads" because they cost money, boosted posts and ads have very different purposes for marketers.

Boosted posts: Think of this as ads for beginners. Essentially, you take an organic post that you know is performing well (because on your Business Page, you can see the performance of every post). Boosted posts work best for actions that are not necessarily associated with sales or hard conversions off-site. Use boosted posts for page likes, comments, shares and general brand awareness. Because these are softer metrics, this is not an area to spend a ton, and it shouldn't be a core part of your strategy. It's an opportunistic choice when you find that a post on your Business Page has done the impossible and gotten a lot of engagement. What do we do when we find a unicorn like that? We get it in front of as many people as possible. If you have a post on your personal profile that drives a lot of engagement, consider using the same post on your Business Page and boosting it, since you know the message is landing.

Facebook ads: Use these when you're looking to make money. The job of a Facebook ad should be to drive prospects into your sales funnel. Whether that's somewhere to download a freebie that leads directly to a paid offer, to purchase a book, or to book a call with you—this channel is focused on hard conversions. Facebook ads that are optimized for conversion take more know-how to set up than a simple boosted post. And again, this is something you should be using once you know you have a message that resonates. When you're ready to set up a Facebook ad, work with a Facebook ads expert or knowledgeable virtual assistant to set this up for you.

Once you are ready to start using Facebook ads, they really can be a game changer to conversions. The truth is, as easy as it is to bash the 'Book for some of their practices, they have developed the single greatest consumer targeting engine in the history of marketing. Not exaggerating. The cost of ads keeps going down as the targeting gets better (Facebook ad impressions increased by 37% in 2019, while the price went down by 6% in the same year).

And the best part? Facebook Ads Manager is how you manage your ads on Instagram too. Yay for efficiency!

My bottom-line Facebook strategy:

- Have a Business page because you need one. Optimize it. Then post on it whenever you remember to.
- Retool your personal profile to connect with your ideal customer instead of friends and family. You can create segmented lists of friends within your profile so you can decide who sees your posts.
- If you already have a Facebook group, make that your primary content hub and put your energy into growing and engaging that group.
- Don't start using ads until you've figured out what works organically.

Instagram

Instagram started as a free photo and video sharing app primarily used on smartphones. Users would upload photos or videos to share with followers, and also view, comment and like posts shared by their friends on Instagram. I remember simpler times when Instagram was all about over-edited photos and branded filters. That was just the beginning.

Since the addition of Stories (a way to compete with Snapchat), IGTV and more recently Reels (to mimic TikTok functionality), Instagram has become the go-to platform for a younger audience, letting them engage in multiple ways.

While it can't boast the same numbers as Facebook, Instagram is a powerful social media platform. The visual-centric property was acquired by Facebook in 2012, and has since taken on the same approach to providing content that matters to users.

With approximately 1 billion users, approximately 37% of US adults use Instagram.

Most popular social networks worldwide as of July 2020, ranked by number of active users (in millions)

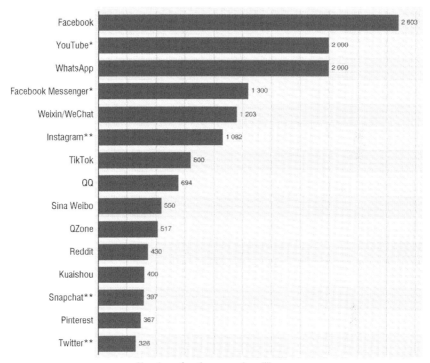

Number of active users in millions

Sources
We Are Social: Various sources (Company data) Hootsuite: Data Reports

Additional Information:
Worldwide: Various sources (Company data) Data Reported as of July 15, 2020, social networks and messenger chat apps

Instagram's population is younger (and slightly smaller) than Facebook, with 18-to34-year-olds making up the bulk of the user base. Also, unlike Facebook, the biggest geographic user base is the United States, followed by India.

Distribution of Instagram users worldwide as of July 2020, by age and gender

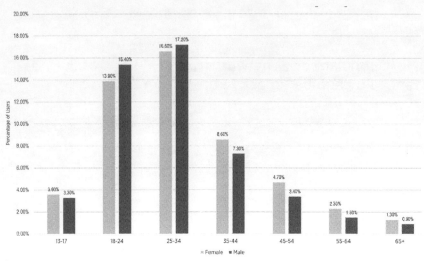

Sources
We Are Social; Hootsuite; Data Reportal; Instagram

Instagram is the world's second most logged-into social media site after Facebook, with 60% of users logging in at least once per day. Instagram users spend an average of 53 minutes on the platform each day compared to Facebook's 58 minutes, according to Recode 2018.

According to Instagram, 90% of its accounts follow at least one brand and 83% of users say they discover new products or services on the platform.

Instagram is also known as the most important platform for influencer marketing (overtaking Twitter and YouTube a few years ago). As an expert who's looking to become an influencer, it makes sense to investigate the possibilities of Instagram and whether its high-visual approach aligns with your offering.

Which social media channels are most important for influencer marketing? (Select multiple)

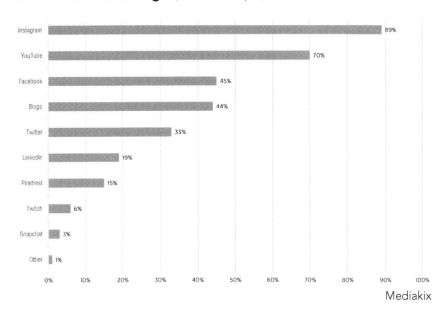

Instagram	89%
YouTube	70%
Facebook	45%
Blogs	44%
Twitter	33%
LinkedIn	19%
Pinetrest	15%
Twitch	6%
Snapchat	3%
Other	1%

Mediakix

Personal vs. Creator vs. Business profile

One of the first choices to make when opening (or reviving) an Instagram account to promote your business is whether to use a personal or business profile.

Do you just want the short answer? Go with the Business profile. If that's enough for you, you can skip to the next section.

Oh, so you want to know why? OK. The Business profile lets you:

- Run ads
- Access post analytics
- Pre-schedule posts
- Connect your account to third-party social media management tools
- Use the native Instagram appointment booking feature

A Creator profile is really for those using the platform to be influencers. It doesn't let you run ads, and doesn't provide the same analytics or functionality. As a Creator, you'll be able to see follow/unfollow data (which isn't a priority metric for a business), tag brands in your posts, and filter your DM inbox. It just doesn't have the firepower. And did I mention, you'll never be able to run ads from a Creator profile?

A Personal profile is exactly what it sounds like. You can post content. You can go private so not everyone can see what you post. That's about it.

Sooooo . . . like I said. Business profile.

Hashtags

While Instagram doesn't have a direct analog to Facebook Groups, hashtags function in essentially the same way for marketers.

A hashtag is the # symbol followed by a combination of letters, numbers, and emojis. Users employ hashtags to categorize their content and make it more findable to those who might be interested in it. Because hashtags are clickable, any user who clicks on an Instagram hashtag (or searches for a hashtag) will see a search results page showing all the posts tagged that way.

Use hashtags to find people who are interested in your area of expertise and posting about it quite a bit. Generally, the goal of using a hashtag in your post is to get that post seen by those following that hashtag. Using hashtags that your ideal client is looking for will help you be discovered by new people.
Instagram has nine categories of hashtags—some broad and some with the potential to be specific. Consider a mix of hashtags from multiple applicable categories.

1. **Product or service hashtags:** General descriptor keywords to describe what it is you do or the service you offer (like #lifecoach or #lawyer)

2. **Niche hashtags:** You can get more specific here and discuss your audience or deeper into what it is that you do (#busymom or #startuplife)

3. **Industry Instagram community hashtags:** Instagram-specific communities for industries or interests(#coachesofinstagram or #doodlesofinstgram)

4. **Special event or seasonal hashtags:** Holidays (real or fake) or seasons (#nationaltalklikeapirateday or #autumndays)

5. **Location hashtags:** Useful if you're looking for people in a specific location but aren't running paid ads to target a specific area (#Omaha, #PDX)

6. **Daily hashtags:** These are exactly what they sound like (#MondayMotivation, #TacoTuesday, #ThrowbackThursday, #SundayFunday)

7. **Relevant phrase hashtags:** More interesting combinations of other categories that describe an experience, activity, phase or event (#onmygrind or #neverthelessshepersisted)

8. **Acronym hashtags:** #TBT for Throwback Thursday, #FOMO for fear of missing out. The thing is you can't just make up your own acronym. They have to be real ones that people actually already know.

9. **Emoji hashtags:** Hashtags that include emojis. Not the best for search and discovery.

As of publication, Instagram allows you to include up to 30 hashtags on a post (only 10 on Stories). For the sake of your followers, try to stick with 1–3 hashtags, never going higher than 10 if absolutely necessary.

Instagram Stories

Instagram developed the Stories functionality to compete with Snapchat. Stories appear in the Stories area for 24 hours and disappear. They're the same dimensions on Instagram as on Facebook, but have higher adoption on IG. About 500 million users (half of Instagram's user base) use Stories daily.

According to Instagram, 62% of users say they've become more interested in a brand after seeing it in Stories. And that makes sense—it's still a far less crowded space than the standard feed for brands. Right now, running ads in Stories give brands more exposure than just running in the standard feed.

Within stories, you can post photos, micro-videos or a series of any combination of the two, and add stickers, text, drawings to get your message across. You still have the option of traditional captioning and hashtags. It's a very flexible tool.

Instagram Stories are more user friendly than their Facebook counterpart. And because of the heavy usage of the feature by IG users, it's worth optimizing posts for both Stories and the traditional feed.

IGTV and Instagram Live

As with all social media platforms, Instagram is prioritizing video above other forms of content. IGTV is Instagram's answer to YouTube. It was initially developed for longer-form videos that would be appropriate for the standard feed. If you're prioritizing Instagram, IGTV is an ideal spot for your pre-produced videos, particularly if you're thinking about something more programmatic like an interview show or regular teaching segment.

Instagram Live has been widely adopted—at the beginning of social distancing measures during the COVID-19 pandemic, usage of the platform surged by 70%, according to Business Insider.

When going live on Instagram, users can tune in to Instagram Live during the broadcast, or watch the replay on Stories for 24 hours afterward. For Stories, the platform will automatically cut your video into 15-second segments and string them together for you.

Once you've completed your livestream, you can now choose to send the replay directly to IGTV, where it will live on indefinitely.

If you're planning to make Instagram your primary distribution platform, live video will be key to your success. If you plan on doing teaching or creating other high-value content live, sending the replay to IGTV will allow you to share that content going forward. Instagram's responsiveness to users has made it a powerful platform for those wanting to create a multimedia experience.

Instagram Reels

Released in August 2020 as an answer to TikTok, Instagram Reels allows users to record 15-second videos set to music and share them in their Stories, the Explore Feed, and in the new Reels tab.

Has this garnered a ton of buzz in the marketing community? Yes! Does that mean it's great for your business? No. If this is something you're interested in, this is definitely something fun to experiment with. Until we see best practices emerge, I don't like the idea of anyone making this the core of their content distribution strategy.

Sponsored posts on Instagram

Much like Facebook, Instagram provides the option to promote existing posts or to run ads. The reasons you would do one or the other mirror what was discussed in the Facebook section. Promoting a post is great when you're looking for more interaction, engagement, general brand awareness, and potentially even visits to an off-platform web page. Running an ad should be done with an eye on hard conversions—downloads, registrations, appointment bookings, and sales.

My bottom-line Instagram strategy recommendation

- Go live like crazy

- Host all your high-value videos in IGTV
- Find 5–10 hashtag communities you belong to and leverage those to find your people
- Once you find successful messaging that gets you the engagement you want, try sponsored posts.

LinkedIn

LinkedIn is the business network. If you're selling to traditional businesses—large, medium, or small—this is your platform.

Once thought of only as a place to find jobs or new recruits, LinkedIn has become a content sharing platform—LinkedIn reported having 15x more content impressions than job postings during 2019. Obviously, recruiters and job seekers still use the platform more than anyone, but the release of LinkedIn's Sales Navigator product is one indicator of the platform's power to connect sellers with the right business buyer. And that's where the strength of LinkedIn comes in.

According to Hootsuite, LinkedIn has approximately 675 million monthly users—more than twice that of Twitter. 61% of LinkedIn users are between the ages of 25–34, making it a younger audience than Facebook overall. The audience skews male at 57%, and most LinkedIn users are college-educated and make more than $75k per year.

In 2019, engagement on LinkedIn increased 50% year over the previous year. And best of all, four out of five LinkedIn users drive business decisions, according to a LinkedIn study.
So when it comes right down to it, LinkedIn is the place to be for B2B sales. It's a less crowded marketplace and the content algorithm isn't working against businesses the way it does on other platforms. Granted, it's decidedly less glamorous. But let's leave the glamour to the fake gurus and get on with doing what works.

Personal profile

The building blocks of LinkedIn are personal profiles. This is your primary profile page where you, in essence, tell your personal brand story. Thanks to LinkedIn's legacy as a job-seeking platform, the profile pages still have the feeling of being a resume on steroids. But there are things you can do to optimize your personal profile to focus on your brand and less on your work history.

- Use your banner: Your LinkedIn banner section is widely underutilized. But it's a powerful piece of real estate because whether on mobile or desktop, when someone visits your profile (as they're more likely to do on this platform) they can't miss it. Use it to promote what you're working on now or to succinctly sum up what it is you do.

- Headline area: Grab that Bite-Sized Brand Bio of yours, and paste it here.

- Maximize your about section: This is a fabulous place for your full Brand Origin Story.

- Featured area: Make sure to feature things that you want people to see first. You can feature posts that you've shared on LinkedIn, articles that you've written on the platform, links to other websites, photos or videos. This is one of the primary visual areas people will first see on your profile, so make it count.

The example below is from the profile page of Christina Jandali, a business and social media coach from Canada. Note how her banner and headline focus on telling exactly who she is and what she does. Her about section provides an abridged brand story, and she's edited her featured area to include two of her most important thought leadership, credibility-building pieces. You have to scroll for quite a while before you get to her past job experience, and until you get there, you're being hit over the head with what she does now and why she'd be great to work with.

Christina Jandali · 2nd

Helping coaches and course creators stand out, get seen and create 6-figure+ profits by hosting a free Facebook group.

Vancouver, Canada Area · 500+ connections · Contact info

Connect | 🔒 Message | More...

Deliver Your Genius: Stand Out From Your...

About

Christina Jandali is a confidence boosting, cash creating Business Growth Strategies who helps online business owners stand out, get seen and create 6-figure profits using the power of Facebook.

She went from being broke and putting groceries back on the shelf to becoming a millionaire in her mid 20's, losing it and rebuilding it over again. After climbing the corporate ladder, she realized she was ready to build her own dream business, not someone else's.

She's a mama of two and you can find Christina running, adventuring outdoors, drinking froo-frooey coffee, and hanging out with her family in Vancouver or in the chilly winter months hiking and poolside in sunny Palm Springs.

She serves on the Forbes Coaches council.

Featured

10 Beliefs Holding Successful Female Coaches Back (And Being Surpassed By Millennials)
Forbes

How To Hack The New Facebook Algorithms And Build A Raving Fan Base
Forbes

In this example, you'll see Gary Vaynerchuk's profile. Again, he uses his banner area to promote his company, his about area to tell his story, and his featured area to promote his website.

VAYNER X

VAYNERMEDIA GALLERY TRACER sasha

| Unfollow | More... |

Gary Vaynerchuk · 2nd   ☒ VaynerMedia

Chairman of VaynerX, CEO of VaynerMedia, 5-Time NYT
Bestselling Author

New York, New York · 4,218,640 followers · Contact info

Highlights

15 mutual connections
You and Gary both know Jeffrey K. Rohrs, Scott Monty, and 13 others

About

Gary Vaynerchuk is a serial entrepreneur, 5x New York Times Best-Selling Author, Chairman of VaynerX, CEO of VaynerMedia, CEO of VaynerSports, and Co-Founder of Empathy Wines. He's a highly sought after public speaker,

as well as a prolific angel investor with early investments in companies such as Facebook, Twitter, Tum ...

Featured

Creative & Production
VaynerMedia.com

It's what achieves measurable results, and we have just the people to do that. From writers and art directors, to a full-fledged photo studio and video team, our second-to-none creative department is all under one roof. Which is so rad...

Company page

For a solopreneur building a personal brand, a Company page on LinkedIn is not necessary. Your personal presence is your most important for content distribution and building your brand. The primary benefit for a Company Page? You can run ads and sponsored InMails. If you have no intention of running ads on LinkedIn, stick to your personal profile.

If you plan on using a company page, here are some best practices for optimizing it:

- Fill out all the things: Upload a logo, write a solid overview (Bite-Sized Brand Bio, anyone?), complete the organizational information including your website, and choose a call-to-action button that sends people to the most important place in your content ecosystem—could be your Facebook group, your website, a sales page, a booking page—whatever the entry to your sales system is.

- Show up: Post 2x per week. Each post should have an image at the very least.

- Video: Video gets 5x the engagement as photo posts. And live video gets 24x. Use it.

- Reshares: If anyone @mentions your company page, reshare it.

- Promote: Add a LinkedIn button on your website so people can follow your page from there. Use your personal profile to promote your business page.

Articles

As part of your Content Goldmine structure, you may be producing blog posts on your website. One of the quirks of LinkedIn is that it favors on-platform articles over links to other websites. When you're wanting to share your blog content on LinkedIn, I recommend creating a LinkedIn article, pasting your blog content in the text area, and uploading the featured image from your blog. You'll get significantly more views of the content by working with the platform's preferences. At the end of your article, add call to action—whether it's to book a call with you, join your Facebook group, download your Content Goldmine, or visit a sales page. Whatever is most important in your sales process at that time should be the call to action.

If you're feeling especially sassy, only paste part of your blog text and link to the blog post below the text so users will click over to view the rest of the article. Either way, you'll get more views by keeping the article content on LinkedIn.

Video and LinkedIn Live

As mentioned above, LinkedIn is HEAVILY prioritizing video in the content feed. Uploaded videos get 5x more views than images with photos. And LinkedIn Live videos blow them all out of the water.

When I say uploaded video, I mean uploaded video. Again, LinkedIn prioritizes content that's native to its platform. Providing a link to a YouTube or Vimeo-hosted video will not give you close to the same number of views as uploading the captioned video file.

LinkedIn Live, however, at the time of publication, is currently in beta, and is by application only. The company seems to be favoring large corporations and influencers, so it's not easy for just anyone to get access. As soon as this feature becomes widely available though, you should make it an absolute priority if LinkedIn is a core distribution channel for you.

Ads on LinkedIn

To be completely honest, LinkedIn used to be terrible when it came to paid marketing. But in the last few years, they've really turned things around. The options they offer are some of the most powerful out there, particularly if you're targeting a particular job title or industry. The most popular for driving conversions for consultants, professional service providers and coaches will be sponsored content and sponsored messages:

- Sponsored content: Much like a Facebook or Instagram feed ad, this shows up directly in the user's LinkedIn content feed. You now have the option to run ads that feature a single image, a video, or a carousel that allows users to scroll through multiple images.

- Sponsored messages: Based on the targeting parameters you set or a specific list you provide, LinkedIn will send an InMail message to the contacts of your choice on your behalf. These have some of the highest conversions available, because there are tight controls around how many sponsored messages a user can receive.

Bottom line: LinkedIn is a fantastic choice if your audience is a traditional business audience. Small businesses aren't making full use of the advertising capabilities, and there's a boatload of potential.

My bottom-line LinkedIn strategy recommendation:

- Optimize your personal profile and your Company page.
- Focus on making connections with your personal profile, seek out your Best. Client. Ever! and do most of your posting there—at least 4x/week.
- Post video at least weekly.
- Post an article weekly.
- Post relevant articles in your industry a few times per week.
- Post 2x/week on your business page.
- Run ads using your Company page to target specific job titles and industries when you have something to sell, and messaging that has tested well in organic.
- Message your Best. Client. Ever! connections to start conversations and offer them a consult.
- If you achieve success filling consults organically and want to accelerate this, look into Sponsored Messages.

Twitter

You know, the fun thing about writing your own book is that you can say whatever you want to. And I want to say that I hate Twitter. I really do.

It is much harder to build a personal following on the platform than it was 5–7 years ago. And it's not a platform that was built for engagement—it was built for spewing. So, yeah. Not a fan.

I am of the opinion that most experts, consultants, professional service providers, and coaches would be best served by using Twitter as a tertiary channel. It is still a firehose, and the links included on Twitter still help boost your domain authority a bit. But I don't believe it is generally worth the time to optimize content for Twitter. If you're using a social media management tool like Hootsuite, Buffer, Planoly, etc., you can simultaneously post to Twitter when you post to your more relevant channel. That's as far as I would take it.

In the United States, Twitter is nowhere near the top when it comes to social media platforms.

BUT . . . for those of you in tech or financial services (who are more interested in talking to colleagues than customers), I'll give you the basic rundown of Twitter demographics and best practices.

Twitter has 330 monthly active users, making it one of the smallest platforms and its growth is projected to remain dead flat for the next 4 years. According to Pew Research, 22% of adults in the US use Twitter, and the most likely age group on Twitter is 18- to 24-year-olds (though they don't use it as much as Instagram, Snapchat or even stodgy old Facebook).

Pew Research also determined that 80% of the content on Twitter is generated by 10% of Twitter accounts. The average Twitter user only tweets twice per month.

Most popular social networks worldwide as of July 2020, ranked by number of active users (in millions)

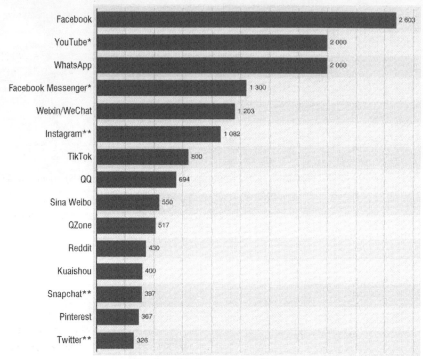

Number of active users in millions

Sources
We Are Social: Various sources (Company data) Hootsuite: Data Reports

Additional Information:
Worldwide: Various sources (Company data) Data Reported as of July 15, 2020, social networks and messenger chat apps

So that should explain why I'm not a big fan of Twitter. If you are on the platform, here are some tips for optimizing your content:

- Once again, video is king. Like every other platform, Twitter prioritizes video. The generally agreed upon the sweet spot for this low-attention-span platform is 6–15 seconds. So depth is not a thing that's necessarily prized here.

- Use relevant and timely hashtags. Twitter basically invented the concept of the hashtag (the only good thing to come out of it) so it's still important to categorize your content. Many Twitter power-users have specific hashtags they look at regularly.

- Obviously, be brief. You may have 280 characters, but that doesn't mean you should use them all. The shorter the better.

My bottom-line Twitter strategy recommendation:

Just don't. At most, just duplicate copy from elsewhere and schedule it here. And if you must make Twitter a part of your strategy, then you need to be there engaging, having conversations, and monitoring like crazy.

Pinterest

Pinterest is an odd duck among the other social media networks... primarily because it doesn't behave at all like a social media platform. It acts much more like a search engine or even a catalog. And while some might dismiss Pinterest as the domain of the perfection-seeking Suburban supermom, hell-bent on creating the perfect themed birthday party for her Sheepa-doodle, it can act as a massively powerful source of traffic to your content. If you're creating content around lifestyle topics like style, cooking, entertaining, fitness, personal growth, parenting, or relationships, Pinterest is absolutely worth exploring.

And here's an unintuitive statistic: Pinterest research says that 89% of Pinners stop by the platform to research financial services products. Who knew?

The reason I didn't include Pinterest as an option in your Minimum Viable Content section is because, as I've mentioned, it is more of a search engine than a true social media platform. The other reason is that Pinterest depends almost entirely on sending users to other content. Knowing that in the Minimum Viable Content stage you may not have off-platform content to send people to, it didn't quite fit the mold.

What we know about Pinterest in 2020, is that it has quietly been growing. Over 2019, the platform experienced 26% growth to reach 335 million monthly users, making it the third-largest social media network in the world after Facebook and Instagram. More than half of those users are on the platform at least once a week. In that same time frame, the platform's revenue grew by 51% (which is insane), showing that advertisers are now seeing the value that Pinterest brings to the table. The number of advertisers on the platform doubled in 2019.

Pinterest is a platform for women, who make up nearly 80% of the platform's user base. High-income households ($75k+) and college-educated individuals are both more than 2x more likely to be Pinterest users.

97% of all searches on Pinterest are unbranded—meaning users are not searching for brands, they're searching for relevant solutions. This is a group that is open to new products, new brands and new experiences if you can meet their needs. And even if your Pin isn't the first place a user lands, if you use a strong keyword strategy, they're likely to find you via related Pins, which accounts for 40% of engagement on the platform.

Like all other platforms, video is carrying heavy weight on Pinterest, with video views jumping by 6x in 2019 over 2018.

Your profile

As a business on Pinterest, you'll want to optimize your Pinterest profile. Include your logo as the profile pic and a cover photo that is highly visual and engaging. It should capture your brand style and share what you do and how you help.

Your bio in Pinterest is limited to 160 characters and would be a great place for your Bite-Sized Brand Bio.

Set up your Boards (essentially folders where you save Pinned content), around your core content themes—this may be more expansive than what you did in your Minimum Viable Content time, but that's a great place to start. It will give people a clear idea of what kind of content you'll be sharing. You can choose up to five boards to feature, which will be more prominently displayed. Upload a branded cover for each board.

Another option to a cover photo is selecting a cover board. This will fill your cover image area with all the pins from a particular board. Making sure all your Pin graphics are hyper-branded will make sure this area is visually cohesive.

Pins

Pins are the building blocks of Pinterest. They're organized within users' Boards. Your pins can link to product pages, blog posts, lead magnet download pages, and infographics. Now that video can be part of your pins, that's an option you'll want to work into your strategy.

When you create Pins (the graphics that are displayed on Pinterest), create them using a 2:3 aspect ratio and include your logo in each Pin. Overlay the image with targeted, short copy that tells the user exactly what the benefit is or the problem that will be solved using the main search term.

Pins live on Pinterest forever. I still have Pins being shared that I posted four years ago. That's the upside. The downside is that you constantly need to be creating fresh Pins, even for existing content. You should be posting multiple Pins per day. Programs like Tailwind and Sprout Social make the management of this somewhat more manageable, but I would absolutely plan on having a VA help with the volume required.

Newly released this summer are Story Pins—Pins that allow you to include up to 20 pages of images and text. These are fantastic if you want to show a series of how-to images to walk someone through a full process. The downside here is that it gives them little incentive to click through to your site, so be sure to end your Story Pin with a strong call to action.

Pinterest SEO

Because Pinterest is more of a search engine than a true social platform, you have to remember to include your most important search terms in your profile (name, bio, description), in your Board names and descriptions, and in your Pins (both the visual and the verbal content). This is how Pinners find your content and how they know it aligns with what they need.

My bottom-line Pinterest strategy recommendation:

Set up your own profile so it's optimized like crazy for your search terms and branded within an inch of its life. Set up your Boards to cover your topics and themes. Then hire a VA to make five pins for your Content Goldmine and every Gold Bar you produce. Then have that VA handle all the scheduling in Tailwind. Check analytics every week. Easy peasy!

CHAPTER 7 - **SUMMARY**

- *Facebook Business Pages are useless for organic posting. You need them to run ads, so open one and optimize it.*

- *Facebook is leaning heavily into Groups and video. Your best engagement will come from Facebook Live.*

- *Instagram has the most functionality of all platforms—live, Stories, Reels, IGTV and the explore feed.*

- *Hashtags are the Groups of Instagram. Find your hashtags and use them to find your people.*

- *LinkedIn cannot be beaten for finding traditional businesses to work with or promoting content to people based on job titles.*

- *Twitter is just the worst.*

- *Pinterest is a search engine, not a social network. And its power is wildly underestimated.*

NOTES

Nurturing and Converting Leads with Email

Email is the deeply unsexy workhorse of the digital marketing world. It's where most conversions happen. It's how you keep in touch with your clients and prospects, year after year. It lets you reach out whenever you have something to share, without worrying about algorithm changes.

In this chapter, we'll talk about a simple way to structure an email program so you can get the most out of the channel that always gives the most back.

So many experts, consultants, and coaches are freaked out by getting their social right, that they totally ignore the only channel they actually own—their email list.

Since the dawn of digital marketing, only one thing has stayed true—the money is in your email list. So grow it, nurture it, and give it all the love you have. If you're there for your list, your list will be there for you.

OK, enough relationship counseling. You get it!

In the Content Goldmine model, your Content Goldmine and a few Gold Bar Content types (webinars, downloadables, etc.) are designed to help you build your email list. And as you may recall from chapter one, that's the whole point of this endeavor. Once you have an email address, you can continually market to that prospect as long as you have permission. If you provide consistent value and don't just pummel them with messages, you can keep that permission for quite a while.

We're going to start by going through the three types of emails that you'll use to build your email program, from most important to least important.

1. Email nurture campaigns

2. Single-subject sales emails/series

3. Email newsletters

Email Nurture Campaigns

Email nurture campaigns are THE single most important piece of email marketing you can implement. A nurture campaign is an automated campaign that follows up with a prospect on a pre-defined timeline based on an action they've taken.

More simply put: It's the messages that auto-send when they download a piece of content.

When one of your Best. Clients. Ever. downloads a content piece from you, they are raising their hand and saying "HEY! I'm interested in this topic and I'm interested in your perspective! Here are my email address and permission to contact me."

What a freaking gift that is!

Someone just said they care about your perspective on a topic? The next step is a no-brainer. Give them your perspective on the topic.

Why are nurture campaigns so important? Because you will never have a warmer or more engaged person than the one who just said: "Yeah, show me what you've got." Automating a smart, prepared way to introduce yourself and your expertise isn't just expected, it would be weird if you didn't.

A nurture campaign usually consists of 5–7 email messages over the course of 10–14 days. The first 3–4 emails are primarily about delivering extra value. Let's say, for example, that someone downloaded your Paleo Pantry Must-Haves Shopping List. You know that they're starting a Paleo eating plan or lifestyle. What other content do you already have that could fit into that nurture and draw this handraiser deeper into your ecosystem?

Maybe your 10 Easy Paleo Dinners blog? Maybe your Best Paleo Snack download? Umm . . . your Content Goldmine? Now you're getting it. And knowing that the contact is just starting on the road down the Paleo path, the offer you want to put in front of her is to purchase your Paleo Perfect mini-course. So here's what that email stream might look like:

1. Fulfillment: Send her the piece she's asked for, and let her know that you'll be emailing even more valuable info on the topic. Ask her to whitelist your email.

2. Introduction: Share your Brand Origin Story as it relates to her topic. Tell her what a Paleo lifestyle has done for you. This is a know-like-trust email. In the PS, let her know what will be coming next.

3. Free high-value content #1: Send a link to the 10 Easy Paleo Dinners blog, along with a little commentary around it. In the PS, mention your mini-course and provide a link.

4. Free high-value content #2: Send a link to your Best Paleo Snack download, plus a video showing one of the snacks getting made and some commentary. In the PS, remind her about the mini-course.

5. Mini-course sales: Make this email all about the Paleo Perfect mini-course.

6. Mini-course reminder: One more email about the Paleo Perfect mini-course, with testimonials.

7. Free high-value content #3: Link to your Content Goldmine and some commentary around it. PS to the mini-course.

This is just one way to put a sequence together, but I bet you can spot the most important element. You're providing VALUE, over and over again. You're being recognized in the inbox as someone who is an expert, and can provide insight on a topic that the contact cares about. Yes, you're selling as you go. But it's never pushy or gross—it's about inviting them to learn even more if they've been interested thus far.

At the beginning of coronavirus quarantine, I released a free download on marketing through the pandemic. Those that downloaded it received a nurture series from me that focused on training on how to handle marketing your small business and content creation in the wake of the insanity they were all experiencing. Here's that series, as an example.

Intro email (after the fulfillment email)

Hey %FIRSTNAME%!

My name is Mary Kate Gulick, and I'm a Content Marketing Coach for people like you—real deal experts, consultants, and coaches who know your field inside and out.

I wanted to take a second and say hello and welcome you to the Real Deal Content community. I'm all about helping professionals with deep expertise figure out how to package that up to deliver to an online audience.

I'm so glad you're here!

I believe that right now, you are one of the most important people in the world.

Seriously.

People need coaches, consultants, experts, and advisors now more than ever. They're isolated. They're losing jobs and don't know their next steps. They're freaking out about money. Their relationships are suffering. Their mental health is vulnerable. The wheels are coming off their nutrition and fitness goals. Their small businesses are hurting and they need strategies to get new clients.

And who should people be calling onto help them through these unprecedented problems? YOU!

That's why I'm incredibly proud and excited to work with experts. People with a deep understanding of their fields. I get the honor of helping coaches, consultants, advisors, and professional service providers every day, empowering you to build content programs that transform more lives.

I mean, c'mon, how much fun is that?

The fact that you signed up for a piece of content shows that you care about getting in front of new clients and bringing them value even before they meet you. It also shows that the depth of content matters to you. You're not interested in just peppering the world with surface-level nonsense.

That means you're my kind of person. And you're in the right place!

Here's what you can expect from me . . .

Over the next week, I'm going to send you some of my most popular resources around how experts, coaches, and consultants are making content choices in the current crisis.

I know this is top of mind for our professional community, so I want to provide you as much value as possible on this.

I do have HEAPS of education on content marketing available to you, but I promise not to overwhelm you in the coming days. We'll start with the situation at hand and tackle how to deal with content in our unprecedented context.

Sounds good? OK!

Here's what you need to do now to get started . . .

STEP 1: Connect with me on social

If you're not already a member of the Real Deal Experts Creating Content Facebook group, you've GOT to join. We have too much fun and learn a whole lot of solid content skills:
https://www.facebook.com/groups/RealDealContent/.

STEP 2: Make sure you're getting all of my emails in your primary inbox by whitelisting this address.

Over the next few days, I'll be sharing some free training content. As new things come up that I think you'd benefit from, I'll share those as well.

But if the emails can't get through, you won't benefit from the free training content. I don't always make some of these items available for free, so please take a second to make sure you can access it.

That's it! I look forward to getting to know you better. In the meantime, enjoy the free training gifts that are coming.

Talk soon,

Mary Kate

P.S. Expect your first bit of training content tomorrow. It's all about humanizing virtual communication with your clients (you're doing just a little of that these days, right??) and my favorite, most cost-effective tools for that.

P.P.S. I've opened up a few time slots to provide free Content Clarity Sessions for experts who want a clearer direction on how to build your brand and attract the right clients with compelling content. <u>Grab your appointment now.</u>

About me email/high-value content #1

Hey %FIRSTNAME%, it's Mary Kate again!

I promised you earlier I'd send through some free training content. At the bottom of this email, you can access my Tools for Humanizing Virtual Client Communication worksheet. Giving you some easy-to-implement strategies for keeping your client comms meaningful during this crisis.

But first, I wanted to introduce myself a little bit more . . .

This is me in one of my favorite spots in downtown Omaha. I'm Midwest to the core, which means I'm a hard worker and have very little patience for fluff and nonsense.

I've spent the last 20 years working for advertising agencies and large corporate marketing departments, creating award-winning content marketing work.

And over that time, I've always done "side work" for professional service providers and consultants.

*It's become clear over the years that this is the work I love and you are the people I love working with. **Experts who are nerdishly deep in their areas of expertise and passionate about sharing that with the world.***

It was always so refreshing to work with people who just wanted results. Those clients weren't tied up in doing things the way they'd always been done, or breaking new ground just to say we were first.

They wanted content programs that worked. That grew the business. That hit the goals!

That's what I wanted, too.

So, I decided to extend my reach, and find more coaches, consultants, and strategists—those experts who were driven to share what they know.

Seriously, you guys are my favorite.

Why? Because of that can-do, entrepreneurial spirit. Because of the stunning depth of what you know. Because there's no silly corporate baggage. And because it allows me to form real partnerships, where we co-create something awesome that gets real results.

So that's my story. As we get to know each other better, I'd love to hear yours.

OK, now that we're not total strangers anymore, on to the free training.

FREE GIFT #1:

This is the strategy sheet I promised to send you.

I think you'll like this one. I know that you (like all of us) have been thrown into mandatory virtual-only communication with your clients. And like all of us, there have been some struggles.

This sheet breaks down my favorite strategies for much richer virtual communications that show your clients that you're there for them, and provide content in a much more powerful way than just dashing out emails.

HINT: Video calls are on the list (duh), but that's just the tip of the iceberg.

You can go and grab it now (no opt-in required) and there's more coming your way tomorrow.

<GRAB THE STRATEGY SHEET BUTTON>

I'll be sending you free training gift #2 tomorrow. You'll love it. It breaks down why NOW (yes, now, during an unprecedented pandemic) is the best time to get your unique skills in front of people.

(Spoiler alert: It's because they need you more than ever, and their problems are bigger than ever before).

I look forward to sharing it with you!

Talk tomorrow,

Mary Kate (MK)

P.S. I'm still offering free 30-minute Content Clarity Sessions to help you get your expertise out into the world NOW when people need it. I would normally charge for this service, so I am doing it for a SUPER limited time. Book a time now.

High-value content #2

Hey there %FIRSTNAME%!

Yesterday, you should have received your first free piece of training content about humanizing virtual communications with clients.

If you missed it, you may want to do a quick search of your inbox for the subject line: Free gift #1 (as promised): Virtual Client Comms Strategies

Got it? OK. Just want to make sure you're squeezing all the goodness out of this relationship!

Alrighty, now on to what's in store for today . . .

FREE GIFT #2: A blog post about what coaches, consultants and professional service providers can do to show up in these crazy times: The world needs you right now. Do NOT stop showing up for people.

Within the blog, you'll also get access to a worksheet to help you think through how to position your offering with the utmost empathy for those who need it right now.

I wrote this because I had been hearing from so many experts, consultants and coaches that now is not the time to market their services, create new content or get in front of new prospects.

And I was like . . . whaaaaat?

People's worlds are falling apart. There's a major need right now for:

- *Mental health counseling*
- *Relationship counseling*
- *Career and life coaching*
- *Business coaching*
- *Leadership coaching*
- *Digital marketing consulting*
- *Brand consulting*
- *Accounting and financial advice*
- *Fitness and nutrition coaching*
- *Parenting coaching*
- *Hobby/recreational instruction*
- *Home improvement*

The list goes on and on. We. Need. HELP. We need your expertise.

And the need just keeps getting more desperate. More people are going to lose their jobs, want to start businesses, need direction in their job hunt, need someone to talk to about their money, relationships, emotional well-being, fitness, nutrition, hobbies, kids, home projects . . . you name it!

With a need so great, how can you NOT share your talents with those who could benefit from it?

Here's a quick video on the topic as well:

<INSERTED VIDEO OF ME TALKING ABOUT HOW THE WORLD NEEDS THEM>

OK, that's it for today. I hope the _blog, worksheet_ and video give you some ideas on how you can help the people who need you right now. Tomorrow, I'll send you free training gift #3: A quick run-down on how to place Facebook ads. Some of you may already be doing this, but most of the coaches, consultants, advisors and professional service providers I talk to are not because they're super intimidated.

And it is a really powerful, cost-effective way to find the people who need you. **And it can also be very simple.**

So, until tomorrow . . .

Mary Kate (MK)

P.S. Don't forget: I still have a few slots left for free Content Clarity Sessions. These are exclusively being held for experts like you who are serious about providing value to prospects and clients at this time. It's my way of serving during the pandemic, and I normally charge $120 for this time. _Schedule time now!_

High-value content #3:

Hey %FIRSTNAME%, it's MK again!

Can I just say how nice it has been to have you as part of the community these last few days?

Sharing some of my favorite training with you has been great.

We have, though, been talking a LOT about what your clients and prospects need in this challenging time. So I have to ask:

What do YOU need right now?

What's scaring you about your business right now? What are the challenges that you just don't feel like you can overcome? What is completely overwhelming you?

For a lot of experts, coaches and consultants, they've got four big things on their mind right now:

1. *Will my new leads just dry up?*

2. *Will my current clients run out of money to use my services?*

3. *Will people think I'm an insensitive jerk-face for putting myself out there right now?*

4. *And last but not least . . . WHERE DO I EVEN START???*

(I hope we've answered #3 by now at least!)

Does this sound like you? As people are losing their jobs, portfolios lose value and fear takes over, are you worried about what that means to you?

I'd be surprised if you weren't.

In times like this, there are two things to focus on—finding YOUR people and showing your value.

To show your value, I'm a MASSIVE believer in producing expert content that only you can produce and sharing it in a systematic way (more on that tomorrow).

But for finding your people fast? Facebook has the easiest to use, most powerful targeting capabilities available to small businesses.

(I'm still waiting for the other social media platforms to catch up!)

And I know a lot of people in our community are intimidated by running Facebook ads (because any task that requires me to use the word "algorithm" is just intimidating by nature).

So that's why I put together this quick video. I take you inside my Facebook account to show you how to set up basic ads.

<INSERTED VIDEO TUTORIAL SHOWING HOW TO SET UP BASIC ADS>

Facebook ads are quick, simple and cheap. They put you in front of YOUR people and teach you a ton about your audience.

I hope you enjoy free training gift #3. Tomorrow's training gift will give you a peek into the how I like to systemize content marketing so it's simple, sustainable and (most of all) effective.

In the meantime, keep being you and bringing your remarkable skills and talent to the world.

Talk soon,

MK

P.S. If you're ready to put together a solid plan on the best way to put your expertise out into the world, set up time with me for a <u>free 30-minute Content Clarity Session.</u> I have a couple of slots left.

I can only offer this free service for a limited time, so when spots are gone, they're gone. This offer will only be available for a few more days.

Content Clarity Session email

Hey %FIRSTNAME%,

Over the last few days, you've had a chance to dive into some fantastic free training. It's probably got you thinking a bit about your own content and how you're using it to put yourself out there.

I can help with this.

You also may have noticed that I've been offering free 30-minute Content Clarity Sessions for this community of experts—coaches, consultants, counselors, advisors, and professional service providers— who want to share their expertise online, build their brands, and develop a larger client base.

I can only keep that offer open for another 2 days.

So what is a Content Clarity Session? So glad you asked!

Before the Content Clarity Session, I'll send you a questionnaire to learn a bit about you, your expertise, and your business. From there, I'll do a bit of investigating on your current content and presence.

During the consultation, we'll talk about your biggest challenges right now. You'll walk away with:

- *A custom roadmap to reach your next goal*
- *At least three actionable steps you can take right now*
- *Recommendations for future learning to push you further*

These free Content Clarity Sessions are new. It is my way of reaching out to help experts, coaches and service-based entrepreneurs during a global crisis. It's been very popular, but I can only dedicate so many hours in a week to free work. I know you understand. :)

So, in 48 hours, I'll close down the offering. If you'd like to chat, please book a time with me before then.

Talk soon,

MK

So you see the pattern? In the beginning, you're all about value, and you just mention your offer. At the end, you focus more on the offer. If you do NOTHING else with email marketing, make sure you build a nurture campaign for each time you're asking for an email address. You can build these in the Mailchimp Standard plan or Active Campaign. There are other tools for small businesses—like Keap/Infusionsoft and HubSpot, but I don't love the price tag for those just starting out.

Single-Subject Sales Emails/Series

Whenever you're releasing a new product or service, or just have open spots on your calendar, it makes sense to email your list and let them know. Make them an offer. It is all about getting in front of people when the timing makes sense to them. So if you're not emailing regularly, you won't be getting in front of them at the right time.

I recommend a single-subject sales email (or series) for:

- Upcoming webinars—even if a prospect is already on your list, this is a great way to more deeply engage them, especially if you'll be doing any selling at the end of the webinar.

- Pre-launch of new products—Give them a sneak peek of what's coming to prime them for the release.

- New product launches—Early bird/charter member pricing.

- Your Content Goldmine—draw them deeper into your area of expertise and acquaint them with your philosophy or approach.

- Times when you need to fill your calendar: Offer free strategy sessions, assessments, etc.

Email Newsletters

I went back and forth about what to call this type of email. I don't love "newsletters," because it makes people think the email itself should look like a newsletter—with sidebars and complex formatting. It shouldn't. It should be a one-column email that reads well on mobile.

The reason it's a "newsletter" is because it contains more than one piece of information. This is your place to provide an update on a few things going on. The main focus should always be on providing value. And the best part is that the bulk of what you include will be content you've already created.

It makes sense to send these out on a consistent cadence . . . you can do weekly, monthly, or even quarterly—just pick a cadence and commit to it. I prefer weekly, because you can become part of a regular routine that way.

Items you can include in your newsletter include:

- A quick note from you on current events/recent developments
- New blog posts, video or podcast episodes
- Upcoming webinars or events
- Latest product/offer
- Booking link

I've listed this as the least important. If you're consistently nurturing your hand raisers and sending out regular single subject emails, you're in decent shape. This is just a way to round out the program and become a regular feature in someone's inbox in a way that provides value.

Think of it this way . . . once someone gets through your initial nurture, it would be great if they hear from you twice a week: once on Monday with your high-value newsletter, and once later in the week with a single subject email. Twice a week is completely respectable—there are digital marketing experts out there who will say if you have an email address, you should hit it every day. I disagree. During a nurture, this may make sense. But overall, people prefer restraint when it comes to their inboxes.

One more word about newsletters: don't use the word "newsletter" in your subject line. Please, in the name of all that is good in the world.

Compelling Subject Lines

If you think back 15 or 20 years ago, subject lines were meant to just tell users what was in the email. And back then, every email got opened, so this helped people prioritize. Now, a subject line determines whether or not the email gets deleted while someone is dinking around on their phone while waiting in line for Chipotle.

Long story short: your subject line is the most important part of your email. If it's bad, the rest of the email doesn't matter because no one will ever see it.

No matter what style subject line you're going for, KEEP. IT. SHORT. I know so many email deployment platforms provide a 60-character recommendation for subject lines. Shoot for 30–35. Get really good at being concise.

When you sit down to write your subject line, don't just dash something out as an afterthought. The job of the subject line is to tell your user what to expect and to get them to open the email. Here are a few tested formulas that can make that happen:

1. **Numbers:** I've spent my entire life marveling at how weird people are. Subject lines prove it. People LOVE numbers, and I don't know why. The subject line "4 ways to get your energy back" will outperform "Get your energy back" every damn time. I don't know why it works, it just does.

2. **Relevant questions:** I've seen a million people recommend question subject lines, then I've seen a million subject line writers put the most pointless questions forth and expect them to work. "Would you like to sleep better?" I sleep fine, thanks. Believe it or not, this email was about how to stress less. If the question had been "What is stress doing to your life?" it would have gotten opened. Make sure the question is at the heart of what's troubling your Best. Client. Ever!

3. **News:** I love a newsy announcement headline because it's simple, it's effective, it's honest, and it appeals to people's desire for novelty. Introducing Mangolo: A new way to track expenses. New updated edition of X book or product. People still like to get the news.

4. **How to:** A "how to" subject line promises value, specificity, and a problem being solved. How to negotiate a raise by Friday. How to hire superstars every time. How to recession-proof your portfolio. How to get your dog to stop peeing on the floor. If you're keyed into the problems that your audience wants to solve, how to subject lines are an efficient, no-nonsense way to do the trick.

5. **Scarcity/urgency:** Yes, they work. But use them sparingly. You don't want to be that person who's always yelling LAST CHANCE!! BUY NOW BEFORE IT'S TOO LATE!! Use real deadlines. Let people know when they're coming up. Use scarcity and urgency when it's really applicable. Remember, you're building a personal brand, not selling hair color on QVC. Show people you respect them.

6. **Personalization:** If your email tool allows you to personalize subject lines, it's a good idea to do this every once in a while. Too often and it feels automated. But used strategically? According to Campaign Monitor, this can boost your open rate by nearly 15%.

7. **Real human talk:** When I'm just checking in with a group of prospects, my subject line might say something like "Just checking in," or "Quick note to see how you're doing." You know, things that actual people might email each other. I do this because I am, in fact, an actual person. And people like to get emails that are a little more real.

Now, you may notice some tactics that are absent from this list. I don't think that click-baity, curiosity gap subject lines do much to build the personal brand of an expert. Yes, if your subject line is "Why your savings aren't going up . . . and it's not the reason you think," your email will get opened. But it feels so cheap. It feels like you're not being totally honest with your people, and that you're trying to manipulate them. You care about the people you're trying to serve. Respect their intelligence as well.

Writing for Email

The word to keep in your mind when writing email is CONVERSATIONAL. You should write like you're speaking to someone. Remember, this is still essentially a 1:1 communication. Treat it like one.

Take a look back at your Brand Voice & Personality. Are you warm, empathetic and genuine? Or are you sharp, quick-witted and no-nonsense? Your strategically chosen voice should guide your language choices everywhere—but they'll be most pronounced in email.

Preheader text: The first piece of email copy to write is your preheader. This is the text that will show up as the preview of your email in mobile email clients. Make sure your preheader complements the subject line and provides a clear, enticing look at what's in the email.

Greeting: Have a "branded" greeting. Maybe you always say, "Hey there, <NAME>!" or "Good day, <NAME>," depending on your brand voice. Use this consistently. It becomes part of the texture of how you communicate.

Body: Whether the body of your email is short or long (both can work equally well), your paragraphs should be short and pithy. Like one paragraph short. Or even one word short. Big blocks of text intimidate people and, consciously or otherwise, push them to delete or ignore the email because they don't want to be bothered with dense reading.

Call to action: No matter what type of email you're sending, it should include a clear action step for the user to take. Whether that's clicking a button to a landing page or blog, setting an appointment with you, or joining a Facebook group, there should be one primary thing that you're asking them to do, and a mechanism for them to do it from the email. While newsletter-type emails may have multiple links, all others should have a single call to action.

Signature: As with greetings, you'll want to brand this. Based on your message and your voice, how do you want to sign off? I've seen:

- Yours in success
- Kiss, kiss
- With grace & gumption
- Your favorite nerd
- Always on your side
- Humbly

Experiment with what is appropriate to your brand, and stick with it.

PS: As much as an anachronism as the post-script is, it is still one of the most-read pieces of text in an email. Crazy, right? So include one. Use it to repeat your call to action or hint at something that's coming up.

CHAPTER 8 - **SUMMARY**

- *Email works better than any other digital channel when it comes to conversion. Be there for your email list and it will be there for you.*

- *Email nurture campaigns are the must-do of email marketing.*

- *Your subject line is the single most important piece of content in your email.*

- *Keep your emails conversational in tone—short paragraphs with a single call to action.*

- *Brand your greeting and signature according to your brand voice and personality.*

NOTES

CONCLUSION

Holy progress, Batman.

We've done a lot over the course of these pages.

You learned the basics of Content Marketing and how you can use it to build your brand and business in a way that's effective, respects your expertise, and establishes your authority.

You learned all about your Best. Client. Ever! The problems she wants to solve, things that keep her up at night, what she's searching, where she hangs out on Facebook, and what your competitors are promising her.

You built out a Real Deal brand messaging strategy! You have a clear definition of your unique Value Proposition, your Positioning within the market, your Content Mission Statement so your ideal audience knows what kind of expertise you share regularly, your Brand Voice & Personality so you sound like YOU and nobody else, your Brand Origin Story to connect with the people who will appreciate you, and your Bite-Sized Brand Bio that you can use all over social media, email and more.

Knowing that you were heading into the heavy lifting of creating a Content Goldmine, you took the time to develop a Minimum Viable Content Experience, so you could start conversations, sharing expertise, and building a following while your major content project was still cooking.

THEN, you really got serious. You dove into the Content Goldmine. You named it, outlined it and (hopefully) started building it out.

You learned how to systematically break down that eBook, research report, or course into Gold Bar Content—regular blog posts, videos, infographics, webinars, worksheets and more so you could generate a regular volume of content without a marketing department or agency.

You made smart choices about the one or two social media platforms you want to be active on, learned about how to succeed on those platforms, and put together a *simple* strategy to promote your content regularly there.

Finally, you learned what to do with all those email addresses you'll be collecting. Why nurturing hand raisers is an absolute must-do to get traction, and how to create emails that serve your audience and your business, without being gross and salesy.

It's a lot. Content Marketing is a lot. But using the concept of one core piece of content—your Content Goldmine—to serve as the engine for all the rest will take you so far. It will give you the volume and consistency to gain real traction and build real authority.

But let's not forget one thing . . . in order to create a Content Goldmine at all, you need Real Deal expertise. Deep knowledge in a subject area coupled with relevant, real-world experience to guide people through their decisions. Without that expertise, nothing I said matters. This approach won't work if you've only got a trick or two up your sleeve.

But I'm not worried about you. You're here because you're the Real Deal. You know your shit, and you want to put it to good use in the world, helping businesses and families get farther along in their journeys.

Your expertise is needed. The transformation it provides is important. Without you, people might find their way to a Fake Guru, get lousy advice, and never get that transformation that they want so desperately. The job of Content Marketing is to put experts like you up to the microphone. The phonies have had their day. I'd like you to help me usher in the era of the expert— Real Deal smarties giving Real Deal advice, effecting Real Deal change in the lives of people who need it.

I'm so proud to have the opportunity to work with experts like you. Thanks for letting me join you on your journey to getting known for what you know best.

ABOUT THE **AUTHOR**

Mary Kate Gulick is a 20-year content marketing veteran with deep expertise in financial and professional services, coaching and consulting. She holds a MA in advertising, marketing and communication studies from the University of Nebraska—Lincoln, is an AMA Professional Certified Content Marketer, a certified Agile Marketing practitioner, and an Adobe Digital Marketing Master. She currently lives in Omaha, Nebraska with her husband, two sons and a Miniature Goldendoodle.

Learn more at MaryKateGulick.com or join the Real Deal Experts Creating Content Facebook Group.

Made in the USA
Middletown, DE
24 September 2021